Passing the PRINCE2 2009 Edition Foundation

CW00524300

Other publications by Van Haren Publishing

Van Haren Publishing (VHP) specializes in titles on Best Practices, methods and standards within four domains:
- IT management
- Architecture (Enterprise and IT)
- Business management and
- Project management

Van Haren Publishing offers a wide collection of whitepapers, templates, free e-books, trainer material etc. in the **VHP Knowledge Base**: www.vanharen.net for more details.

VHP is also publisher on behalf of leading organizations and companies:
ASLBiSL Foundation, CA, Centre Henri Tudor, Gaming Works, Getronics, IACCM, IAOP, IPMA-NL, ITSqc, NAF, Ngi, PMI-NL, PON, Quint, The Open Group, The Sox Institute

Topics are (per domain):

IT (Service) Management / IT Governance	Architecture (Enterprise and IT)	Project/Programme/ Risk Management
ABC of ICT	Archimate®	A4-Projectmanagement
ASL	GEA®	ICB / NCB
BiSL	SOA	MINCE®
CATS	TOGAF®	M_o_R®
CMMI		MSP™
CoBIT	**Business Management**	P3O
ISO 17799	CMMI	PMBOK® Guide
ISO 27001	Contract Management	PRINCE2®
ISO 27002	EFQM	
ISO/IEC 20000	eSCM	
ISPL	ISA-95	
IT Service CMM	ISO 9000	
ITIL® V3	ISO 9001:2000	
ITSM	OPBOK	
MOF	Outsourcing	
MSF	SAP	
SABSA	SixSigma	
	SOX	
	SqEME®	

For the latest information on VHP publications, visit our website: www.vanharen.net.

Passing the PRINCE2® 2009 Edition Foundation exam

A Study guide

Bert Hedeman

Gabor Vis van Heemst

Steffi Triest

Colophon

Title:	Passing the PRINCE2® 2009 Edition Foundation exam – A Study guide
Series:	Best Practice
Authors:	Bert Hedeman (Hedeman Consulting) Gabor Vis van Heemst (Intrprimus) Steffi Triest (Semcon Project Management)
Text editor:	Steve Newton
Reviewers:	Pierre Bernard (Pink Elephant Canada) Eddie Borup (ibp Solutions) Hans Fredriksz (ISES)
Publisher:	Van Haren Publishing, Zaltbommel, www.vanharen.net
ISBN:	978 90 8753 622 0
Print:	First edition, first impression, June 2011
Layout and typesetting:	CO2 Premedia, Amersfoort – NL
Copyright:	© Van Haren Publishing 2011

Contents

1 About this book

The purpose of this book is to provide guidance to the readers in order to gain a basic understanding of the PRINCE2 method and to pass the PRINCE2 Foundation exam. For the content of the method this book has been based on the manual 'Managing Successful Projects with PRINCE2™'. This is a publication of the OGC, Office of Government Commerce. For the exam specifications this book has been based on the exam syllabus: *Managing a Successful Project using PRINCE2® - Syllabus 2011*. For the Foundation examination candidate guidance we have made use of the publication *PRINCE2 Foundation exam - Candidate Guidance V1.2*. These two are publications of the APM Group Ltd.

This book starts with the performance definition of a Foundation candidate and the examination format from the syllabus. Thereafter all fifteen syllabus areas are described per learning objective. In Appendix A.1 a glossary is included, together with examination guidance, a multiple choice answer key, and relevant publications and contact addresses.

1. About this book
2. Introduction to the syllabus
3. Overview, principles and tailoring PRINCE2 to the project environment
- **Section I Themes**
  4. Business Case
  5. Organization
  6. Quality
  7. Plans
  8. Risk
  9. Change
  10. Progress
- **Section II Processes**
  11. Starting up a Project
  12. Directing a Project
  13. Initiating a Project
  14. Controlling a Stage
  15. Managing Product Delivery
  16. Managing a Stage Boundary
  17. Closing a Project
- **Appendices**
  G1 Glossary
  G2 Foundation examination candidate guidance
  G3 Multiple choice answer key
  G4 Organizations
  G5 References
  G6 About the authors

Structure of the chapters

The chapters covering the syllabus areas follow a standardized structure. First the purpose of the syllabus section is given, there then follows a summary of the learning objectives, the essential definitions, an introduction to the syllabus area and thereafter the description of the individual learning objectives. Finally a set of sample multiple choice questions are given at least one for each learning objective. The answer keys are given in Appendix A.3.

Spelling of the PRINCE2 terms

PRINCE2 recognizes specific management products and roles. For the purpose of identification, these products and roles are always written with a capital letter: for example Executive and Business Case. In addition all PRINCE2 processes are also written with a capital letter. Activities within a process, however, are not characterized by a capital letter.

2   PRINCE2 syllabus

Introduction

The *PRINCE2 2009 – Syllabus V1.1* provided by the APM Group provides exam candidates a breakdown of all the learning objectives that are tested in both the PRINCE2 Foundation and Practitioner exams. However, this book focuses on the Foundation level and, therefore, only information that is relevant to pass that exam is given.

The structure of this book follows the structure of the syllabus since it should form the basis of any learning materials and therefore will be explained further. We have included here the information given in the separate publication of APM Group, *PRINCE2 Foundation Exam Candidate Guidance*.

Performance definition of a successful candidate for the Foundation examination

The Foundation examination will measure whether a candidate could act as an informed member of a project management team on a project using PRINCE2. Candidates need to show that they understand the principles and terminology of the method, and that they specifically understand:
- The purpose and responsibilities of all roles;
- The seven principles, the seven themes and the seven processes, the product-based planning and the quality review technique;
- Which management products are input to, output from and updated in the seven processes;
- The purpose of all management products and the composition of the Business Case, Product Descriptions, Issue Report and the Issue, Risk and Quality Registers;
- The relationship between the principles, processes, themes, products and roles within a PRINCE2 project.

The examination takes one hour and consists of 75 multiple choice questions which cover all 15 areas of the PRINCE2 Foundation syllabus. The exam is a closed book exam. No support material is permitted.

> One hour
> 75 questions
> Multiple choice
> 50% pass mark*
> Closed book

Learning outcome assessment model

APMG has incorporated the Bloom´s Taxonomy of Educational Objectives (Bloom et al.; 1956) into the Learning Outcomes Assessment Model, which is used as a basis for developing the exam qualification scheme and syllabuses. The adaption of the generic model uses a four-step learning level. Levels 1 and 2 represent the Foundation level. Levels 3 and 4 are relevant for the Practitioner examination only and not applicable for the Foundation:

Table 2.1 Four-step learning level

1. Knowledge	Able to recall manual facts, including terms, concepts, principles, themes, processes, and responsibilities.
2. Comprehension	Understands the principles, processes, themes, the project's environment and roles, and can explain how these are applied on or involved with a project.
3. Application	Demonstrates application of the method through: • appropriate use of themes; • creation of management products; • ability to apply appropriate tailoring of the processes and themes
4. Evaluation	Ability to evaluate the use of the method through appraisal of completed products and project events for a given project scenario.

Syllabus areas

The following syllabus areas and associated abbreviations for the syllabus areas are used:

Table 2.2 Syllabus areas

Syllabus area Acronym	Syllabus area
OV	Overview, Principles and Tailoring PRINCE2 to the project environment
BC	Business Case theme
OR	Organization theme
QU	Quality theme
PL	Plans theme
RK	Risk theme
CH	Change theme
PG	Progress theme
SU	Starting up a Project process
DP	Directing a Project process
IP	Initiating a Project process
SB	Managing a Stage Boundary process
CS	Controlling a Stage process
MP	Managing Product Delivery process
CP	Closing a Project process

For each syllabus area the respective learning outcomes and topics as specified in the PRINCE2 2009 – Syllabus V1.1 are given.

Table 2.3 Learning outcomes, levels and topics

Learning outcome (topic header)	What you will have to know, understand or do in order to demonstrate competency in that topic for each level of examination.
Level	Classification of the learning outcome against the APMG Learning Outcome Assessment Model.
Topic	Aspects that a candidate has to master to demonstrate that a learning outcome has been achieved for the Foundation level.

3 Overview, principles and tailoring PRINCE2 to the project environment

Learning outcomes

Syllabus area	Topic	Topic description	Level
Know facts, terms and concepts relating to the overview, principles and tailoring PRINCE2 to the project environment. Specifically to recall the:			
OV	01	Six aspects of project performance to be managed	1
OV	02	Definition of a project	1
OV	03	Four integrated elements of principles, themes, processes and the project environment upon which PRINCE2 is based	1
OV	04	Customer/supplier context of a PRINCE2 project	1
Understand terms and concepts relating to the overview, principles and tailoring PRINCE2 to the project environment, and explain how these are applied on/are involved with a project. Specifically to identify the:			
OV	05	Benefits of using PRINCE2	2
OV	06	Seven principles	2
OV	07	Characteristics of a project	2

Definitions

- **Project** – A temporary organization that is created for the purpose of delivering one or more business products according to an agreed Business Case.
- **Project management** – The planning, delegating, monitoring and control of all aspects of the project, and the motivation of those involved, to achieve the project objectives within the expected performance targets for time, cost, quality, scope, benefits and risks.
- **PRINCE2** - A method that supports some selected aspects of project management. The acronym stands for PRojects IN a Controlled Environment.

Introduction

Project management is increasingly becoming a profession. In the past project management was a task taken on in addition to regular work, whereas nowadays project management is a separate profession from which many people earn a living. However, despite the increased levels of professionalism, projects still frequently fail. Some failed projects hit the headlines, but most are never heard of again. There is no simple reason why projects fail, but a lack of an effective method for managing projects is one of the major causes.

An effective project management method helps the Project Manager to organize and manage a project in a continually changing environment while still involving all the stakeholders. PRINCE2 is such a method and uses the fundamental principles of good project management.

PRINCE2 stands for 'Projects in a Controlled Environment' and is the de facto project management standard in the UK government. Throughout the world PRINCE2 is being used increasingly as *the* method to manage projects.

The method is generic, resulting in it being independent of the type of project. It creates a clear distinction between the specialist and the management aspects within projects. Consequently the method is easy to use and can be simply introduced as a standard within organizations.

The OGC (Office of Government Commerce) holds the copyright to the PRINCE2 brand and to the PRINCE2 methodology, but the method can be used freely.

Definition of a project (OV02)

It is important to recognize the difference between a project and 'business as usual'. Lack of clarity as to what a project actually is can lead to a lot of friction and frustration.

In the context of the above, PRINCE2 describes a project as:

> *A temporary organization that is created for the purpose of delivering one or more business products according to an agreed Business Case.*

A temporary organization entails staff temporarily being assigned to a different set of responsibilities and authority. Business products are products or services that provide added value for the customer. A Business Case is a justification for initiating and delivering a project. In a Business Case the anticipated benefits and estimated costs for the project are recorded, as well as the time over which the benefits will be realized.

Characteristics of a project (OV07)

Projects differ to business as usual in the following ways:
- **Change** – Projects are the means by which change is introduced. Therefore projects always have to deal with the changes in the client organization.
- **Temporary** – This is a distinguishing feature of projects. Projects have a defined start and end date. The project finishes as soon as the pre-agreed products and/or services have been delivered and handed over to the customer.
- **Cross-functional** – The different competencies have to work together in one team from different perspectives and motivations, from both the customer and the supplier side.
- **Unique** – Every project is different because every change is different; the output or the objectives differ; the people involved differ. No two projects are the same.

- **Uncertainty** – All the previous characteristics cause extra threats and opportunities. Projects typically encounter more risks than business as usual.

Customer/ supplier context of a PRINCE2 project (OV04)

PRINCE2 is based on a customer/supplier environment. This assumes that there is always a customer who wants to receive a specific output and a supplier who wants to deliver that specific output. The supplier can be part of the same organization as the customer, but may also be an external party.

The Project Manager is, by default, from the client organization. However, the role of the Project Manager can also be fulfilled by an external contractor or a representative of the supplier.

Six aspects of project performance to be managed (OV01)

Within PRINCE2, project management is defined as the planning, delegating, monitoring and control of all aspects of a project and the motivating of all parties involved to achieve the project's objectives within the agreed performance targets for time, costs, quality, scope, benefits and risks (see figure 3.1).

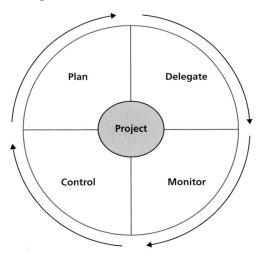

Figure 3.1 Cycle of project management

These six control aspects have to be managed by the Project Manager in each project:
- **Time** – This refers to the total lifecycle of the project including the handing over of the end result.
- **Costs** – This refers to the total costs of creating the project products, including the project management costs.
- **Quality** – Staying within budget and delivering on time is not enough. The end result also has to be fit for use and fit for purpose.

- **Scope** – What is the total scope of the project? What is exactly to be delivered and what not? What work has to be done and what does not?
- **Risks** – Every project has a degree of uncertainty and therefore contains risks. In itself this is not a problem, as long as it is managed well. Managing the threats - as well as the opportunities - is thus an absolute must.
- **Benefits** – Perhaps the most important questions in projects are 'why are we doing this?', 'what are we trying to achieve by doing this?', 'what advantages can be gained from the end result?' and 'are the costs still in the right proportion to the anticipated benefits?'.

Four integrated elements of principles, themes, processes and the project environment upon which PRINCE2 is based (OV03)

The PRINCE2 method is based on four integrated aspects of project management:
- **Principles** – The fundamental principles and best practices to which any given project must comply if it is to be a PRINCE2 project.
- **Themes** – The minimum management aspects that must be managed by the Project Manager throughout the project. Each theme describes the specific application and its necessity.
- **Processes** – The processes describe the entire lifecycle of the project step-by-step, from starting up to closure. Each process describes the requisite activities, management deliverables and related responsibilities.
- **Tailoring to suit the project environment** – PRINCE2 cannot be successful until it is applied 'sensibly'. Adjusting the method to the type of project and the project environment is, therefore, crucial.

PRINCE2 does not provide:
- **Specialist aspects** – This is also one of the strengths of the method. As a result of this, PRINCE2 can be applied to any type of project.
- **Detailed techniques** – Except for product-based planning and quality review no techniques are described within the method, as all the other common techniques are well documented or industry-specific.
- **Leadership** – Leadership, motivation and other social skills are immensely important, but cannot be addressed in one method. However, through the structure of the method, PRINCE2 supports leadership within the context of the project.

Seven principles (OV06)

PRINCE2 offers a project management method independent from the specific characteristics and the context of a project. This is possible due to the fact that PRINCE2 is based on a number of principles that a project must satisfy and not on a prescribed set of procedures and templates.

These principles have been shown to be effective over the years, and they are universal and can be used in any project. These principles also serve to motivate the users of the method, because it offers them the opportunity to organize and tailor the project in terms of specific characteristics and context. For a PRINCE2 project, however, the application of these principles is not optional. If you do not think and act from the perspective of these principles, you cannot call it a PRINCE2 project!

1. Continued business justification

For every PRINCE2 project there must be a business reason to commence it. This reason is the project's business justification and is indispensable as a foundation for making decisions with regard to the project. Although the business justification can change during the course of the project, it will still have to remain valid and thus be tested continually. This justification is set down in the Business Case, formally approved and then subjected to formal change control.

2. Learn from experience

PRINCE2 project team members learn from experience. Lessons are not only sought but also recorded and applied during the project. Project management is a profession. It is a trade that must primarily be learned by applying it.

3. Defined roles and responsibilities

A PRINCE2 project has clearly defined roles and responsibilities organized in such a way that the interests of the business, user and supplier are represented. A temporary organization is required for the purpose of delivering the result, including the accompanying tasks, responsibilities and authority. These can sometimes be profoundly different to the normal rules and cultures within the business as usual organization.

4. Manage by stages

A PRINCE2 project is divided into stages. It provides the opportunity to direct the project on a step-by-step or stage-by-stage basis. Each stage boundary provides a formal checkpoint, allowing approval of the (interim) products already assessed as well as detailed planning of the next stage on the basis of this. Working in stages also provides the Project Board with the opportunity to assess the viability of the project and to ensure control of the progress by means of predefined decision points.

5. Manage by exception

Effective governance can be achieved by allocating unequivocal responsibilities and authority to the respective levels of governance. The advantage of working with the principle of management by exception is that the next higher level of management is only involved in the governance of the project if there is a specific reason for doing so. For the Executive this will only be at decision points agreed in advance, if advice and direct intervention is required, or if there is a risk of agreed tolerances being exceeded. This principle provides the Project Manager with some flexibility, limits the number of meetings and eliminates the need for the Executive and other members of the Project Board to be involved in operational matters. If it is anticipated that tolerances will be exceeded, escalation to the next higher management level is required.

6. Focus on products

According to PRINCE2, results-oriented working is a fundamental principle for projects. You cannot define the work to be carried out if you do not know what to deliver. The total of the project products defines the scope of the project: what is and what is not to be delivered and whether this meets the expectations.

7. Tailoring to suit the project environment

PRINCE2 can be used irrespective of the nature of the project and irrespective of the context within which the project is being implemented. A direct consequence is that the method does have to be tailored to be used 'sensibly', i.e. not slavishly sticking to prescribed activities and products, but also not ignoring every suggestion or recommendation in the method. Tailoring ensures that the project management method is in line with the organization's project processes and that the project controls are based on the project features and environment.

Benefits of using PRINCE2 (OV05)

PRINCE2 is a methodology that, thanks to its continuous application, has developed to a mature level with many benefits. Here is a summary of the most important of these:

- PRINCE2 is proven best practice and widely recognized;
- Provides a common vocabulary and approach, and can be applied to any one project;
- Focuses on management aspects only and can be integrated easily with industry-specific standards;
- Management by exception for senior management;
- Focuses on continuous justification of the project;
- Clear roles and responsibilities for all participants and involvement of users and suppliers;
- Focuses on what the project will deliver to the management of business and project risks;
- Plans meet the needs of different levels of management;
- Allocates resources as part of the go/no go decision moments;
- Based on meetings that only take place if they are essential and uses economical structure of reports;
- Incorporates quality control during the whole lifecycle of the project;
- Promotes learning and continuous improvement;
- Promotes the reuse of project assets and facilitates staff mobility;
- Availability of accredited training organizations;
- Facilitates assurance and assessment of project work;
- Is a diagnostic tool for assurance and assessments.

Multiple choice - Introduction

OV01. Which of the following describes a project the best?
a. Driven by the output to be delivered
b. Driven by a vision of the 'end state'
c. Has a predefined path
d. Is an ongoing endeavour

OV02. Which of the following is NOT a characteristic of a project?
a. Cross-functional
b. Unique
c. Uncertain
d. Repeatable

OV03. Which of the following describes the context of a PRINCE2 project the best?
a. Based on a customer/supplier environment
b. Based on a customer/user environment
c. Based on a customer/client environment
d. Based on a stipulated Business Case

OV04. Which of the following are aspects of project performance that need to be managed according to PRINCE2?
a. Scope, Tolerances, Stakeholder, Controlling, Monitoring
b. Time, Costs, Quality, Scope, Risks, Benefits
c. Planning, Reviewing, Tracking, Reporting
d. Risk, Costs, Quality, Benefits, Soft skills

OV05. Identify the missing words in the following sentence.
[?] are the four integrated elements upon which PRINCE2 is based.
a. Business Case, Plans, Controls, Quality
b. Scope, Time, Cost, Risk
c. Principles, Themes, Processes, Tailoring
d. Specialist aspects, Leadership, Techniques, Benefits management

OV06. Which of the following is NOT one of the seven PRINCE2 principles?
a. Learn from experience
b. Tailoring to suit the project environment
c. Defined roles and responsibilities
d. Focus on change

OV07. Which of the following is NOT one of the benefits of using PRINCE2?
a. Common vocabulary
b. Availability of accredited training organizations
c. Focus on what the project will deliver
d. Availability of a tailored leadership methodology

I   PRINCE2 themes

The PRINCE2 themes describe those aspects of project management that have to be addressed continuously and integrally throughout the lifecycle of every project (see figure I.1).

Figure I.1 PRINCE2 themes

- **Business Case** – To establish mechanisms that assess whether it is, or remains, desirable, viable and achievable to start or continue with the project.
- **Organization** – To define and establish the project's structure of accountabilities and responsibilities.
- **Quality** – To define and implement the resources by means of which the project will be able to produce and assess products that are fit for purpose.
- **Plans** – To define the scope and the means of delivering the products.
- **Risks** – To identify, assess and control uncertainties, thereby improving the capacity of a project to be successful.
- **Change** – To identify, assess and control any potential and approved change to the baseline.
- **Progress** – To monitor and compare actual achievements against those planned so that a forecast can be provided on the project objectives to be fulfilled, and to enable any unacceptable deviations to be controlled.

4　Business Case

Purpose (BC02)

The purpose of the Business Case theme is to establish mechanisms to judge whether it is, or remains, desirable, viable and achievable to start or continue with the project.

Learning outcomes

Syllabus area	Topic	Topic description	Level
Know facts, terms and concepts relating to the Business Case theme. Specifically to recall the:			
BC	01	Definition of a project output, outcome, benefit and dis-benefit	1
Understand how the Business Case theme relates to the principles; the approach to the treatment of this theme; how it is applied throughout the project lifecycle and the responsibilities involved. Specifically to identify:			
BC	02	The purpose of the Business Case theme	2
BC	03	The purpose of a Business Case and Benefits Review Plan	2

Definitions

- **Business Case** – The information that reflects the justification for the setting up and execution of a project.
- **Output** – A specialist product that is delivered to the user(s).
- **Outcome** – The result of change, normally described in terms of the way in which it affects real-world behavior and/or circumstances.
- **Benefit** – The measurable change that is indicated positively by one or several stakeholders.
- **Dis-benefit** – The measurable change which is deemed negative by one or more stakeholders.

Introduction

The Business Case provides the business justification for a project. It is essential to know how the project's costs relate to the returns, what the Executive is aiming to achieve with the project outputs and how great the risks are in this regard. If the costs and risks do not weigh up against the expected benefits, then there is no valid Business Case and there is no reason to start or continue the project.

The Senior User is responsible for specifying and subsequently realizing the benefits through the use of the project output. The Executive is responsible for assuring that the specified benefits represent value for money in respect of the project costs and risks, and are aligned to the corporate or programme objectives.

How the Business Case relates to the principles

The Business Case theme supports the continued business justification principle by:
- Establishing, developing and maintaining the mechanism for the Business Case;
- Describing the recommended composition of the Business Case;
- Setting the basis upon which to judge whether the project is, or remains, desirable, viable and achievable.

Definition of a project output, outcome, benefit and dis-benefit (BC01)

Within this framework it is important to use an unambiguous conceptual framework. An output is the product or service that is delivered by a project. An outcome is the effect of that output within the client organization and/or wider environment. A benefit is the measurable change resulting from the outcome which is deemed positive by one or more stakeholders. And ultimately a dis-benefit is the measurable change as a result of an outcome which is deemed negative by one or more stakeholders.

PRINCE2 approach to the Business Case theme

The Business Case has to be developed prior to and/or at the outset of the project and has to be maintained during the project's lifecycle. The Project Board will have to assess the Business Case during the go/no go decision points, such as at the end of a stage. Finally, the benefits to be achieved in the Business Case will have to be tested and confirmed during the benefits reviews (see figure 4.1).

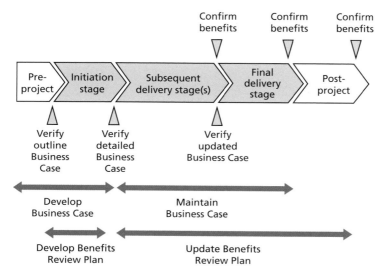

Figure 4.1 Developing the Business Case (based on OGC PRINCE2 material)

Alongside the development and maintenance of the Business Case, a Benefits Review Plan will also have to be developed, maintained and assessed. The Benefits Review Plan forms a basis for assessing the Business Case and measuring the benefits forecast.

In a project lifecycle it is possible for some project outputs to be delivered during the project i.e. at the end of a stage, and not just at the end of the project. In these cases the benefits from the early project deliverables can be assessed, perhaps even as early as during the next stage. The benefits reviews can even be part of the work that has to be carried out in the project. However, achieving these benefits always falls outside the scope of the project.

The purpose of a Business Case and Benefits Review Plan (BC03)

The purpose of the Business Case is to document the justification for undertaking a project. The purpose of the Benefits Review Plan is to define how and when a measurement of the achievement of the project's benefits, expected by the Senior User, can be made.

Roles and responsibilities for the Business Case theme

See table 4.1 for a description of the roles and responsibilities for the Business Case theme.

Table 4.1. Roles and responsibilities for the Business Case theme

Corporate / programme management	Project Manager (PM)
• Provide mandate and define any standards for development of the Business Case • Hold Senior User to account for realizing the benefits • Accountable for Benefits Review Plan (post-project)	• Prepare the BC on behalf of the Executive • Conduct impact analyses on issues and risks that may affect project's viability • Assess and update the BC at the end of each management stage • Assess and report on project performance at project closure
Executive • Own Business Case for duration of project • Approve Benefits Review Plan • Ensure alignment of project with business strategies • Secure funding	**Project Assurance** • Assist in development of the BC • Ensure viability of BC is constantly reassessed • Monitor changes to the Project Plan to identify any impact on the BC • Verify and monitor BC against issues and progress • Review impact assessments on Project Plan and BC • Monitor project finance on behalf of the customer • Ensure project stays aligned with corporate or programme strategy • Verify and monitor Benefits Review Plan for alignment to corporate or programme management
Senior User • Specify the benefits upon which the BC is approved • Ensure the desired project outcome is specified • Ensure that project produces products which deliver the desired outcomes • Ensure the expected benefits are realized • Provide actual versus forecast benefits statement at benefits reviews	
Senior Supplier • Approve supplier's Business Case (if any) • Confirm that the products required can be delivered within expected costs and time	**Project Support** • Keep the Business Case under configuration • Advise PM about changes that may affect the BC

Multiple choice - Business Case theme

BC01. Which of the following is NOT part of the defined purpose of the Business Case theme?
a. To judge whether the project remains viable
b. To judge whether the project should be continued
c. To identify how, and by whom the project's products will be controlled
d. To check whether the project should be started

BC02. What is an aspect of the Business Case theme that supports the continued business justification principle?
a. Establishing developing and maintaining the mechanism for the Business Case
b. Describing the recommended composition of the Benefits Review Plan
c. Setting the basis to judge whether the budget for the project should be extended
d. Defining and capturing the respective targets and tolerances

BC03. Which statement correctly defines output?
a. The product or service that is delivered by a project
b. Measurable change as result of the outcome
c. A certain event occurring in the future
d. An uncertain event that, if it occurs, should be escalated to the Project Board

BC04. Which statement correctly fits with the PRINCE2 approach to the Business Case theme?
a. Where there is a staged handing over of the project outputs, the benefits of the project can fall within the project scope
b. Measurement of benefits always falls outside the project scope
c. A Business Case has to be updated at stage ends only
d. At the end of the project the Business Case has to be updated

BC05. Which statements are correct in regard to a Benefits Review plan?
1. The plan is presented to the Executive during the Initiating a Project process
2. Updated at each stage boundary
3. Is used to define how and when a measurement of the achievement of the project's benefits can be made
4. Used by the Controlling a Stage process when assessing the impact of issues and risks
  a. 1, 2, 3
  b. 1, 2, 4
  c. 1, 3, 4
  d. 2, 3, 4

BC06. What is NOT a responsibility of the Executive in relation to the Business Case theme?
a. Verify and monitor the Business Case against issues and progress
b. Ensure the desired project outcome is specified
c. Define any standards for development of the Business Case
d. Approve the Benefits Review Plan

5 Organization

Purpose (OR02)

The purpose of the Organization theme is to define and establish the project's structure of accountability and responsibilities.

Learning outcomes

Syllabus area	Topic	Topic description	Level
Know facts, terms and concepts relating to the Organization theme. Specifically to recall the:			
OR	01	Roles within the Organization theme	1
Understand how the Organization theme relates to the principles; the approach to the treatment of this theme; how it is applied throughout the project lifecycle and the responsibilities involved. Specifically to identify:			
OR	02	The purpose of the Organization theme	2
OR	03	The three project interests and how these are represented within the project management team structure	2
OR	04	The responsibilities and characteristics of the roles within the project management team	2
OR	05	What a stakeholder is	2
OR	06	The purpose of the Communication Management Strategy	2

Definitions

- **Customer** – The person or group who commissioned the work and will benefit from the results.
- **Supplier** – The person or group(s) responsible for the supply of the project's specialist products.
- **User** – The person or group(s) who will use one or more of the project's specialist products.
- **Stakeholder** – Any person, group or organization that can affect, be affected by, or perceive itself to be affected by, an initiative.

Relations to the principles

The Organization theme directly relates to the:
- Defined roles and responsibilities principle as it defines the organizational structure and roles for the project.

- Manage by exception principle as it establishes the project's structure of accountability and responsibilities.
- Tailoring principle, as it defines roles which can be assigned to different persons/functions to suit the project environment.

The Organizational theme directly contributes to all the other principles as well, since accountability and responsibilities for these principles are defined within the Organizational theme.

PRINCE2 approach

Different people in different functions or jobs can hold different positions within a project. Therefore, the Organizational theme describes defined roles rather than functions or jobs.

The three project interests and how these are represented within the three levels of the project management team structure (OR03)

In each project there are always three primary categories of interests:
- **Business** – The person, group or organization on whose interests the project is funded and who will need a justification for the investment.
- **User** – The person, group or organization that will use one or more of the project's specialist products.
- **Supplier** – The person, group or organization responsible for the supply of one or more of the project's specialist products.

The term 'customer' is the collective term for the business and user interests in a project.

The three levels of management within the project management team structure are:
- **Directing** – The Project Board is responsible for directing the project. It reports to the corporate or programme management regarding the success of the project and is accountable for the project within the mandate.
- **Managing** – The Project Manager is responsible for the day-to-day management of the project. The prime responsibility is to ensure that the project's specialist products will be delivered within the time, costs, scope, quality, risk and benefits tolerances set by the Project Board.
- **Delivering** – The Team Manager is responsible for supervising the specialists and producing the specialist products on time, within budget and according to the quality standards set.

Roles within the Organizational theme (OR01)

The roles within the Organizational theme are (see figure 5.1):

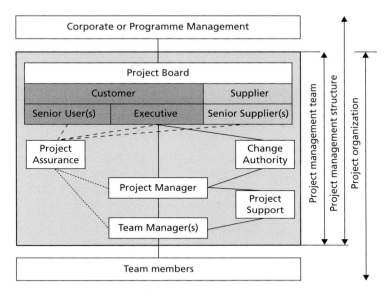

Figure 5.1 Project management team structure (based on OGC PRINCE2 material)

The responsibilities and characteristics of the roles in the project management team structure (OR04)

Project Board – Comprises the roles of Executive, Senior User and Senior Supplier, and is the project's decision-making body. It is important that each of the members truly has the authority to make decisions on behalf of the group they are representing.

The members of the Project Board are appointed by the corporate or programme management. They have to bring unequivocal direction and leadership to the project, make the required resources available and provide unambiguous decision-making.

The Project Board must assure that the project stays within the agreed tolerances and that the products are delivered in accordance with the agreed specifications. Finally, the Project Board must ensure that there is effective communication, both within the project and with external stakeholders.

In some cases, the role of the Executive and Senior User, or the role of Executive and Senior Supplier can be combined. From the perspective of the customer-supplier relationship, it is not possible to combine the roles of Senior User and Senior Supplier.

Executive – Is accountable for the project and the owner of the Business Case. As the chairman of the Project Board, the Executive takes the final decisions. The Executive must ensure that the project delivers 'value for money' and that the objectives as specified in the Business Case can be fulfilled via the output of the project. In this regard, the Executive has to try and maintain equilibrium between the interests of the customer, the users and the suppliers.

The Executive is accountable for setting up an effective project organization and the formation of planning, and needs to take the accompanying decisions. The Executive needs to communicate or escalate these decisions to the corporate or programme management. It is the Executive who formally closes the project and discharges the Project Manager. The Executive chairs the benefits reviews and communicates the outcome to the stakeholders. The role cannot be shared. Therefore there can be only one Executive on a Project Board.

Senior User – Represents the interests of the users. The Senior User is responsible for ensuring that the specifications and accompanying acceptance and quality criteria are defined unequivocally and in full, and that the product is fit for purpose. From the perspective of the users, the Senior User is responsible for ensuring that the products are tested to the appropriate quality standards and methods, and should indicate which users will be involved in the tests.

The Senior User is also responsible for communicating with the users or their management, and for the deployment of people and resources at his/her end. He/she will have to make the final decision about conflicting interests among the users. Usually the Senior User is designated as Change Authority within the Project Board.

This role is responsible for identifying and defining the benefits and for demonstrating to the corporate or programme management that benefits are being achieved as forecasted. The role can be filled by several persons. Alternatively, the organization may choose to have a user forum and select one member to represent it on the Project Board.

Senior Supplier – Represents the interests of those people designing, securing, producing and implementing the output of the project. The Senior Supplier is responsible for ensuring that the specialist products are being produced in accordance with the agreed criteria. In drawing up the product specifications, the Senior Supplier is responsible for checking the technical feasibility. In addition to this, the Senior Supplier contributes to the creation of the planning and the estimating of the costs and is responsible for freeing up sufficient resources to achieve the output of the project in accordance with specifications and within budget and planning. The role of Senior Supplier can be filled by several people. A supplier forum can be put together, from which one member is sent to the Project Board to represent it.

A representative from purchasing or procurement can take on the role of Senior Supplier in the early stage of the project when the external supplier to the project is not yet selected.

Project Assurance – Represents the responsibility of the individual members of the Project Board in order to provide reassurance to the Project Board that the agreed deliverables are being developed. This task can take up a lot of time and often requires specific qualities and is therefore usually delegated to one or more persons outside the Project Board. The members of the Project Board continue to be accountable for this supervision, however.

The role of Project Assurance for the Executive is often filled by someone with a finance background as they have responsibility for the Business Case. The Senior User role is often filled by the customer's Quality Manager, whilst the Senior Supplier role is often filled by a Controller and the supplier's Quality Manager.

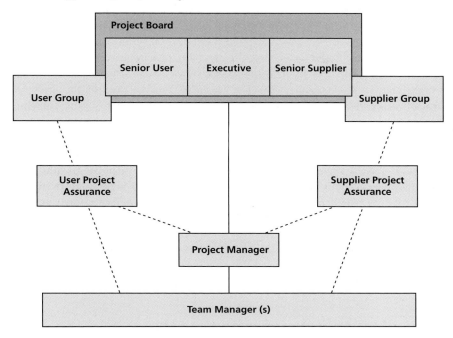

Fgure 5.2 Possible reporting structures using user and supplier forums

Members of the user and supplier forums can take up the role of assurance in the project or can support Project Assurance (see figure 5.2). The role of Project Assurance cannot be combined with the role of Project Manager.

Change Authority –The Change Authority is the person or group to whom the Project Board has delegated the responsibility to assess, authorize and deal with change requests and off-specifications within the agreements made on these items.

Often a Senior User is the Change Authority. However, even the Project Manager can be authorized as a Change Authority, or the role can be allocated to people or groups from the corporate or programme management, such as a Change Advisory Board.

Project Manager – Is responsible for the day-to-day direction of the project within the tolerances as these have been agreed with the Project Board. In this regard, the Project Manager is responsible for planning the work, authorizing the Work Packages, monitoring progress and taking corrective action. If the agreed tolerances are at risk of being exceeded, the Project Manager must escalate this to the Project Board using an Exception Report.

It is the primary responsibility of the Project Manager to ensure that the project produces the agreed products, in line with the agreed standards of quality, on time and within budget. Although the Project Manager is not responsible for accomplishing this ultimate situation, he/ she has to ensure that the Business Case in question is still realistic. The role cannot be shared. Therefore there can only be one Project Manager on a project. Furthermore the role of Project Manager cannot be combined with the role of Executive.

Team Manager – Is responsible for producing the specialist products. Team Managers are responsible for the Managing Product Delivery process and, therefore, for the production of one or more specialist products in accordance with an agreed Work Package based on the approved Stage Plan. The role is optional. The Project Manager can decide to direct the work personally.

Project Support – Is the responsibility of the Project Manager. However this role can be delegated to a separate entity. This could be one of the project staff, a supporting department within the Project Management Team, or a department set up for this purpose within the corporate or programme organization. This responsibility encompasses (among other things) the administrative support, together with advice and guidance in the use of project management procedures and templates and any applications. Administrative handling of the configuration management procedures, in particular, falls under the remit of Project Support.

Within some organizations a permanent Project Office has been set up that can take over part of the Project Support's tasks for a project.

How the Organizational theme is applied throughout the project lifecycle

The corporate or programme management issues the project mandate which triggers the start of the pre-project stage as described in the process Starting up a Project. In this process the corporate or programme management appoints the Executive. The Executive in turn appoints the Project Manager, and this appointment has to be confirmed by the corporate or programme management. The Project Executive and Project Manager design and appoint the project management team, including the applicable role descriptions.

In the initiation stage the project management team will be updated, based on the results of the preparation of the individual strategies. As part of this stage the role of Project Assurance and Change Authority may be assigned.

At the stage boundaries the project management team may be updated to meet the requirements of the next stage and to adapt to the changing conditions within which the project operates.

The corporate or programme management must confirm all changes to the Project Board including any change of the Project Manager. The Project Board must confirm all changes to the project management team.

At the closure of the project a recommendation should be raised by the Project Manager to the Project Board to issue a project closure notification and release the resources. The Project Executive releases the project management team. Ultimately the corporate or programme management releases the Project Executive.

What a stakeholder is (OR05)

Any person, group or organization that can affect, be affected by, or perceives itself to be effected by a project is a stakeholder of the project. These are the members of the project management team itself, as well as persons and groups within the supplier and client organizations and within the wider environment, such as clients of the customer, unions, industry regulators and outsiders affected by the project results (see figure 5.3).

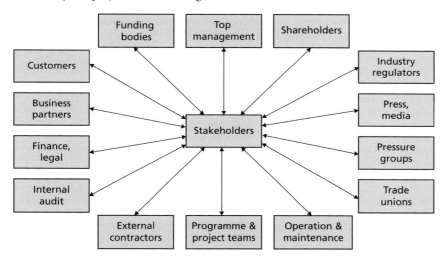

Figure 5.3 Possible stakeholders of a project

The project decision-makers within the project management team are the members of the Project Board. The Executive is the key project decision-maker within the board. The respective corporate or programme management takes the ultimate decisions about the project.

Purpose of the Communication Management Strategy (OR06)

In the initiation stage of the project a Communication Management Strategy is prepared to manage the effect on stakeholders of the project and of stakeholders on the project. It contains a description of the means and frequency of communication to parties both internal and external to the project. It establishes the engagement of the stakeholders to the project via a controlled two-directional flow of information.

Roles and responsibilities for the Organization theme

For an overview of the roles and responsibilities for the Organization theme, see table 5.1.

Table 5.1 Overview of roles and responsibilities for the Organization theme

Corporate / programme management	Project Manager (PM)
• Provide project mandate • Appoint Executive and PM (optional) • Confirm approval of (updated) PID and Benefits • Review Plan, review (updated) Business Case • Provide information as defined in CMS • Decide on exceeded project tolerances • Accept hand-over project product • Discharge Executive	• Day-to-day management of the project • Ensure project produces the required products within the specified tolerances • Design, review and update the PMT and role descriptions • Produce and update the necessary management products (in general) • Establish and manage project's procedures & controls • Prepare, review and update the CMS • Lead and motivate project management team • Liaise with corporate or programme management and any external supplier/account manager • Manage the information flow/ communications • Authorize Work Packages • Perform Team Manager and/or Project Support role, unless appointed to another person(s)
Executive • Owns the problem / Business Case • Secure funding for project • Design and appoint PMT • Approve (external) supplier contract • Keep project in line with business strategy • Direct & monitor progress at strategic level • Organize and chair Project Board meetings • Hold SU and SS to account • Balance demands of SU and SS • Manage key stakeholders at strategic level • Manage strategic risk/issues • Ensure overall business Project Assurance	**Team Manager (TM)** • Prepare Team Plan and accept Work Package • Advise on project team members and stakeholder engagement • Plan, monitor and manage team work • Ensure quality activities are performed and the appropriate entries in Quality Register are made • Produce Check Point Reports • Identify and advise PM on issues and risks associated with the Work Package • Liaise with Project Assurance and Project Support • Deliver the Work Package to the PM
Senior User (SU) • Specify user needs and acceptance criteria • Brief management on supplier aspects • Resolve user requirements/conflicts • Approve changes (optional) • Ensure user resources • Communicate with users • Ensure output meets user requirements • Ensure expected benefits are realized • Ensure user Project Assurance	**Project Assurance** • Advise on PMT and stakeholder engagement • Assist PM with Business Case and Benefits Review Plan • Ensure right people are involved in writing Product Descriptions and performing reviews • Assess and advise on management products • Ensure methods/procedures are correctly followed • Ensure liaison with stakeholders is effective • Monitor risks and issues to the project • Assess solution is still fit for use and fit for purpose • Assess progress is within tolerances
Senior Supplier (SS) • Assess and confirm viability of project • Brief management on supplier aspects • Resolve supplier requirements/conflicts • Ensure proposals delivering output are realistic • Ensure supplier resources • Ensure supplier quality procedures • Ensure supplier Project Assurance	
CMS = Communication Management Strategy PMT = Project Management Team	**Project Support** • Provide administrative support to PMT • Maintain Quality and Configuration Item Records • Update plans • Administer Project Board meetings • Contribute expertise in tools and techniques

Multiple choice - Organization theme

OR01. What is the purpose of the Organization theme?
a. To define the project in order to form the basis for its management
b. To give a summary of progress to date
c. To manage by stages
d. To define and establish the project's structure of accountability and responsibilities

OR02. Which of the following is a principle that the Organization theme does NOT contribute to?
a. Manage by exception
b. Tailor to suit the project environment
c. Define roles and responsibilities
d. Thought leadership

OR03. Which of the following best describes the approach of the PRINCE2 Organization theme?
a. Based on function and roles
b. Based on functions and jobs
c. Based on roles rather than functions
d. People have fixed roles in projects

OR04. Which of the following is NOT one of the three project interests?
a. Business
b. Customer
c. Supplier
d. User

OR05. What is NOT a defined role in the PRINCE2 project management team structure?
a. Project Support
b. Configuration Manager
c. Change Authority
d. Project Assurance

OR06. Identify the missing words in the following sentence.
Often a Senior User is also the [?]
a. Change Advisory Board
b. Project Assurance
c. Change Authority
d. Team Manager

OR07. Who needs to confirm changes in the project management team?
a. Project Board
b. Corporate or programme management
c. Project Manager
d. Team Manager

OR08. Who is the key project decision-maker in the project management team?
a. Change Advisory Board
b. Executive
c. Corporate or programme management
d. Project Board

OR09. Which of the following is NOT a correct statement about the Communication Management Strategy?
a. Contains a description of the means of communication
b. Prepared in the Initiation Stage
c. Is used to document the justification for the undertaking of a project
d. Contains a description of the frequency of communication

OR10. What is NOT a responsibility of the Project Assurance?
a. Ensure the right people are involved in writing Product Descriptions
b. Advise on stakeholder engagement
c. Monitor risks and issues to the project
d. Specify user needs and acceptance criteria

6 Quality

Purpose (QU02)

The purpose of the Quality theme is to define and implement the resources through which the project will be able to produce and assess products that are fit for purpose.

Learning outcomes

Syllabus area	Topic	Topic description	Level
Know facts, terms and concepts relating to the Quality theme. Specifically to recall the:			
QU	01	Recommended quality review team roles	1
Understand how the Quality theme relates to the principles; the approach to the treatment of this theme; how it is applied throughout the project lifecycle and the responsibilities involved. Specifically to identify:			
QU	02	The purpose of the Quality theme	2
QU	03	The difference between quality assurance and Project Assurance	2
QU	04	The objectives of the quality review technique	2
QU	05	The difference between quality planning, quality control and quality assurance	2
QU	06	The difference between customer's quality expectations and acceptance criteria	2
QU	07	The purpose of: • Project Product Description; • Product Description; • Quality Register; • Quality Management Strategy.	2

Definitions

- **Quality** – The totality of features and inherent or assigned characteristics of a product, person, process, service and/or system that bears on its ability to show that it meets expectations or satisfies stated needs, requirements or specifications.
- **Scope** – The sum total of the project's products and the extent of their requirements.

Introduction

The Quality theme describes the PRINCE2 approach to ensuring that the project delivers products that fulfill the customer quality expectations and enable the desired benefits to be subsequently achieved.

Further the Quality theme describes the quality methods, procedures and responsibilities for specifying, developing, completing and approving the specialist products and the management products.

Finally, the Quality theme describes the quality cycle of continuous improvement within the project and within the relevant existing organizations by recording, applying and passing on lessons. In so doing, the Quality theme contributes directly to the principle of learning from experience.

Relations to the principles

The focus on product principle is central to the Quality theme. By addressing the implementation of continuous improvement, the Quality theme supports the learning from experience principle.

PRINCE2 approach

The PRINCE2 quality approach is focused on identifying all the products needed and to be realized, defining the respective Product Descriptions, and implementing and tracking the quality methods to be employed throughout the project. Identifying and defining the products are covered by the quality planning. The implementation and tracking components are covered by quality control and quality assurance.

The difference between quality planning, quality control and quality assurance (QU05)

The purpose of quality planning is to provide an effective baseline for quality control, Project Board agreement and communications to project stakeholders. The quality planning comprises:
- Understanding of the customer's quality expectations; defining the project's acceptance criteria and documenting these in the Project Product Description;
- Defining the Quality Management Strategy;
- Writing the individual Product Descriptions;
- Creating the Quality Register.

The purpose of quality control is to ascertain that the quality criteria are met, by controlling the process of realization and the products to be delivered, and identifying the causes of mistakes and unacceptable performance. Quality control comprises:
- Carrying out the quality activities;
- Maintaining quality and approval records;
- Updating the Quality Register;
- Gaining acceptance of the project product.

The purpose of quality assurance is to ascertain that the quality requirements can be fulfilled. Quality assurance is a process-oriented approach, most familiar in the form of the Deming Cycle, developed by Dr. W. Edward Deming: Plan – Do – Check – Act. Quality assurance comprises an independent check and recording that the quality planning and the quality control organization and processes are in place.

The difference between quality assurance and Project Assurance (QU03)

Within PRINCE2, quality assurance is defined as being a responsibility of the corporate and programme management, whereas quality planning and quality control are responsibilities of the project management team. Quality assurance can also be the function within the corporate or programme management that establishes and maintains the quality management system.

Quality assurance deviates in this from Project Assurance. Project Assurance is the defined responsibility of the Project Board to ascertain that the project is conducted properly in all aspects. Of course both assurances contribute and overlap with each other. For the differences and relationship between Project Assurance and quality assurance see table 6.1.

Table 6.1 Relationship between Project Assurance and quality assurance

Project Assurance	Quality Assurance
Assurance to the project's stakeholders that the project is being conducted appropriately and properly and complies with the plans and standards agreed	Assurance to the corporate or programme management that the project is conducted appropriately and properly and complies with the relevant corporate or programme standards and policies
Must be independent of the Project Manager and project team	Must be independent of the project management team
Responsibility of the Project Board	Responsibility of the corporate or programme organization
Corporate or programme quality assurance function can be used by the Project Board as part of the Project Assurance regime (e.g. to conduct quality audits)	Proper Project Assurance can provide confidence that the relevant corporate or programme standards and policies are met

The difference between customer's quality expectations and acceptance criteria (QU06)

The customer's quality expectations form a record of the quality expectations of the customer in order to create a common understanding about the quality of the project product and the activities needed to realize and to assure the quality of that product. The customer's quality expectations comprise:
• The key requirements for the project product;
• Standards and processes to be applied within the project to meet the quality requirements

and to what extent the customer or supplier quality management systems are used within the project;
• Any metrics to be used to assess whether the quality requirements will be met.

Acceptance criteria form a prioritized list of criteria that the project must meet to be acceptable for the customer, for instance measurable definitions of attributes for the products to be handed over (see table 6.2).

Table 6.2 Example of quality expectation and acceptance criteria

Quality expectation	Acceptance criteria
Key requirements	Measurable definition of attributes
Small	Less the 192 cm

The customer's quality expectations and acceptance criteria are defined and agreed in the Starting up a Project process, and captured in the Project Product Description.

The purpose of different quality management products (QU07)

Project Product Description - The purpose of the Project Product Description is to record what the project must deliver in order to obtain the customer's acceptance, and with that to record the project's scope and requirements.

The Project Product Description is created in the Starting up a Project process as part of the Project Brief. In the Initiating a Project process the Project Product Description is updated and captured in the Project Plan.

Product Description - For each identified product a Product Description must be prepared. The purpose of a Product Description is to create a common understanding of the product by recording:
• The detailed nature, purpose and functions of the product;
• Who will need the product;
• The sources from which input is needed to realize the product;
• To what quality criteria the product must be realized;
• The activities and people or skills required to produce, review and approve the product.

A Product Description must be prepared as soon as the product is identified, even if only in a rudimentary form. A Product Description should be baselined as soon as the respective Stage Plan is approved.

Quality Register - The Purpose of the Quality Register is to record all the quality management activities that are planned or have taken place, to provide information about the status of the quality activities and specifically:

- To issue a unique reference for each quality activity;
- To act as a pointer to the quality records for a product;
- To act as a summary of the number and type of quality activities undertaken.

The Quality Register is created in the Initiating a Project process. The Quality Register is updated with the planned quality management activities as soon as the respective Stage Plan is approved. During the Controlling a Stage process the Quality Register will be updated with the actual quality results.

Quality Management Strategy - The purpose of the Quality Management Strategy is to record the quality techniques and standards to be applied, and the responsibilities for achieving an effective quality management procedure.

The Quality Management Strategy is developed by the Project Manager in the initiation stage and is approved as part of the Project Initiation Documentation by the Project Board during authorization of the project. This Strategy is evaluated and (if necessary) updated, at a minimum, at the end of each management stage.

The objectives of the quality review technique (QU04)

A quality review technique is a structured procedure performed by a team of people to assess the conformity of a product with a set of quality criteria. The technique is designed to assess whether a product that takes the form of a document or similar, is complete, adheres to the standards and meets the quality criteria agreed for it in the respective Product Description.

The core of the review is a meeting in which those involved must form a collective opinion of the product and how to proceed. In the quality review, the emphasis is on recording errors and improvements and not on solving the problems on the spot.

The objectives of a quality review are:
- Assessing the conformity of the product against the quality criteria;
- Involving all key interested parties in checking the product's quality and promoting acceptance;
- Providing confirmation that the product is complete and ready for approval;
- Creating a baseline for change control.

Recall the recommended quality review team roles (QU01)

The recommended team roles for a quality review are:
- **Chair person** – Responsible for performing the entire review process.
- **Presenter** – Introduces the product into the review on behalf of the people that have produced the product, and is also the person responsible for dealing with any corrective action. Often the Team Manager is the presenter.
- **Reviewer(s)** – Assessing the product from the perspective of their specific expertise or interest.
- **Administrator** – Providing administrative support and taking the minutes of the review meeting.

Roles and responsibilities for the Quality theme

For an overview of the roles and responsibilities for the Quality theme, see table 6.3.

Table 6.3 Roles and responsibilities for the Quality theme

Corporate / programme management	Project Manager (PM)
Corporate / programme management • Provide corporate/programme Quality Management Strategy • Provide quality assurance **Executive** • Approve Project Product Description • Approve Quality Management Strategy • Confirm acceptance of project product **Senior User** • Provide customer quality expectations • Provide acceptance criteria • Approve Project Product Description • Approve Quality Management Strategy • Approve Product Description for (key) user products • Provide user resources for quality activities • Communicate with user stakeholders • Provide acceptance of project product **Senior Supplier** • Approve Project Product Description • Approve Quality Management Strategy • Approve quality methods, techniques & tools • Approve Product Description for key specialist products • Provide supplier resources for quality activities • Communicate with supplier stakeholders	**Project Manager (PM)** • Document customer quality expectations and acceptance criteria • Prepare Project Product Description • Prepare Quality Management Strategy • Prepare and maintain Product Descriptions • Ensure TMs implement agreed quality control measures **Team Manager (TM)** • Implement agreed quality control measures • Produce products consistent with Product Descriptions • Manage quality controls for Work Package products • Assemble quality records • Advise PM about product quality status **Project Assurance** • Advise Project Board and PM on Quality Management Strategy • Assist Project Board and PM by reviewing Product Descriptions • Advise PM on suitable quality reviewers • Assure PB on implementing strategies **Project Support** • Provide administrative support for quality controls • Maintain Quality Register & quality records • Assist with project quality processes

Multiple choice - Quality theme

QU01. What is the purpose of the Quality theme?
a. To define and implement the resources through which the project will be able to produce and assess products that are fit for purpose
b. To define and establish the project's structure of responsibilities
c. To define the project in order to form the basis for its management
d. To provide an effective baseline for quality control

QU02. How is the learning from experience principle supported by the Quality theme?
a. By creating a Lessons Log
b. By providing the Project Assurance role
c. By covering the implementation of continuous improvement
d. By archiving the Lessons Log in the Quality folder

QU03. What does quality control NOT include?
a. Maintaining quality and approval records
b. Defining the Quality Management Strategy
c. Gaining acceptance of the project product
d. Carrying out the quality activities

QU04. Who is responsible for Project Assurance?
a. Project Board
b. Project Manager
c. Team Manager
d. Corporate or programme management

QU05. What are the customer's quality expectations used for?
a. To ascertain that the quality criteria are met, by controlling the process of realization and the products to be delivered
b. To provide an effective baseline for Project Board agreement and communications with project stakeholders
c. To create a common understanding about the quality of the project product
d. To record the responsibilities for an effective quality procedure

QU06. The Project Product Description is?
a. A record of all project products with detailed planning
b. A record of what the project must deliver in order to be accepted by the customer
c. A record of what the general approach for the project will be
d. A record of all strategies regarding the products to be delivered

QU07. Which of the following statements is NOT correct in relation to the quality review technique?
a. Should be used for every product
b. A structured procedure
c. To assess the conformity of a product with a set of quality criteria
d. Performed by a team of people

QU08. Who are the members of the quality review team?
1. Chairperson
2. Presenter
3. Senior Supplier
4. Administrator
   a. 1, 2, 3
   b. 1, 2, 4
   c. 1, 3, 4
   d. 2, 3, 4

QU09. What is NOT a responsibility of the Senior User within the Quality theme?
a. Provide all resources for the quality activities
b. Provide customer quality expectations
c. Communicate with stakeholders
d. Provide acceptance of project product

7   Plans

Purpose of the Plans theme (PL03)

The purpose of the Plans theme is to facilitate the implementation, communication and control of the output by defining the means of delivering the products.

Learning outcomes

Syllabus area	Topic	Topic description	Level
Know facts, terms and concepts relating to the Plans theme. Specifically to recall the:			
PL	01	Levels of plans recommended by PRINCE2	1
PL	02	Four tasks of product-based planning	1
Understand how the Plans theme relates to the principles; the approach to the treatment of this theme; how it is applied throughout the project lifecycle and the responsibilities involved. Specifically to identify:			
PL	03	The purpose of the Plans theme	2
PL	04	The purpose and the interrelationship between the Project Plan, Stage Plan, Team Plan and Exception Plan	2
PL	05	The tasks within the product-based planning technique	2

Definitions

- **Plan** – A detailed proposal for achieving a result or an aim which specifies who undertakes what, where, when and in what way.
- **Record** – A dynamic management product that maintains information regarding project progress.
- **Report** – A management product providing a snapshot of the status of certain aspects of the project.
- **Specialist product** – A product whose development is the subject of the plan.
- **Management product** – A product that will be required as part of managing the project, and establishing and maintaining quality.

Introduction

To a significant extent, project management is based on designing and developing a plan. Without a good plan, there is no common idea regarding the work to be carried out, there is no basis upon which the work's progress can be measured and there is no basis for managing the implementation.

The Planning theme describes the framework for designing, developing and updating the various plans in a project.

In the PRINCE2 approach, preparing a plan is product-based. You cannot define the work to be carried out if you do not know what to deliver.

Relations to the principles

The Plans theme contributes directly to the principle of focus on products by defining the purpose, quality criteria, method and responsibilities for each of the project's products.

The Plans theme contributes directly to the principle of manage by exception by defining and capturing the respective targets and tolerances.

The Plans theme contributes directly to the principle of manage by stages by defining separate Project and Stage Plans. Further, the management stages are captured in the Project Plan.

PRINCE2 approach

PRINCE2 distinguishes three levels of plans: for the Project Board, the Project Manager and the Team Manager.

When preparing a plan the principle focus is on the product; first and foremost it must be clear what has to be delivered and in what order, before the requisite activities can be planned. This defines the steps to produce a plan.

To define the products required and the order in which they have to be delivered, PRINCE2 recommends four specific tasks. A product-based planning technique is described to carry out these tasks properly.

Levels of plans recommended by PRINCE2 (PL01)

PRINCE2 distinguishes three levels of plans to satisfy the needs of the various management levels in the project. Each planning level must tie in with the next higher planning level. The Project Plan has to tie in with the corporate or programme plan. The Stage Plan has to tie in with the Project Plan. The Team Plan has to tie in with the Stage Plan (see figure 7.1).

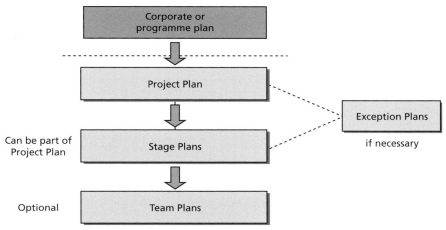

Figure 7.1 Levels of plans recommended by PRINCE2

The purpose and the interrelationship between the Project Plan, Stage Plans, Team Plans and an Exception Plan (PL04)

The Project Plan - is the baseline for the Project Board to monitor and direct the project stage-by-stage. The Project Plan outlines how the project product will be realized within the given objectives of time, money, scope and quality, the agreed management stages and the most important deliverables, activities, milestones and required resources within the timeframe.

The Project Plan is prepared by the Project Manager in the initiation stage and is approved by the Project Board as part of the Project Initiation Documentation. Prior to the end of each intermediate management stage, the Project Plan is updated and approved with the authorization to proceed with the next stage. During the Closing a Project process, the Project Plan is updated using the details as a basis for preparing the End Project Report.

The Project Plan provides input for the Business Case with regard to the necessary investments and the period over which these investments have to be made.

A Stage Plan - serves as the baseline for the Project Manager for the day-to-day management of the relevant stage. A Stage Plan describes the products to be delivered and the Work Packages to be implemented during a stage. The Stage Plan is prepared by the Project Manager and approved by the Project Board.

A Stage Plan is required for each individual management stage. For that reason there are at least two Stage Plans: the Stage Plan for the initiation stage and the Stage Plan for the delivery stage. If there is only one delivery stage then the relevant Stage Plan can be amalgamated with the Project Plan.

The Initiation Stage Plan is prepared at the end of the starting up stage. The Stage Plan for the initial delivery stage is prepared at the end of the initiation stage. The Stage Plans for the other management stages are prepared as part of the Managing a Stage Boundary process at the end of the previous management stage. This enables a Stage Plan to be produced within the period for which it is possible to plan accurately (the planning horizon) and to use the knowledge gleaned from the achievements in earlier stages.

A Team Plan - describes the deliverables and the work to be carried out in order to be able to implement and deliver the relevant Work Packages. A Team Plan is prepared by the Team Manager and must be approved by the Project Manager in the project and by the Senior Supplier in the line (outside of the project).

A Team Plan is not arranged in a set way. Suppliers do not necessarily work based on the PRINCE2 method and this may result in other arrangements of such plans.

A Team Plan can be prepared by the Team Manager, at the same time as the Project Manager is preparing the Stage Plan, or as part of the activity accept a Work Package, during the Managing Product Delivery process.

The Team Plan is optional. Sometimes the Stage Plan is worked out in such detail that individual Team Plans for the respective Work Packages are not necessary. If no separate Team Plan is prepared for the various Work Packages, then the relevant Team Managers will have to be involved more emphatically in preparing the Stage Plan.

An Exception Plan - is a plan that describes what is needed to correct the effects of exceeding the tolerances or the resulting threats. In terms of arrangement, an Exception Plan is the same as the plan it is replacing, and in terms of timeframe it relates to the time left for the plan it is replacing.

The Project Board must approve the replacement of a Stage Plan by an Exception Plan. The corporate or programme management must approve the replacement of a Project Plan by an Exception Plan.

Four tasks of product-based planning (PL02)

Product-based planning should be used for defining and analyzing the products (see figure 7.2). Firstly the Product Description of the project product has to be written. Based on that, the product breakdown structure can be drafted. Thereafter the Product Descriptions of the individual products can be written. Finally the product flow diagram can be created.

The tasks within the product-based planning technique (PL05)

Write the Project Product Description

The Project Product Description is the overall Product Description for the final product. The Project Product Description is prepared during the Starting up a Project process, to specify what has to be delivered (the project product).

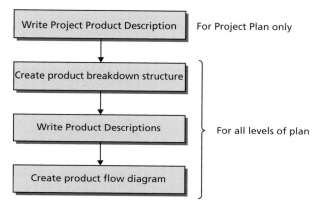

Figure 7.2 The tasks within product-based planning technique (source: Managing Successful Projects with PRINCE2, produced by OGC)

The Senior User is responsible for specifying the project product. In practice, the Project Product Description is written by the Project Manager in consultation with the Executive and the Senior User.

Create the product breakdown structure

The project product to be realized usually consists of several products that have to be completed, assessed and delivered separately. To prevent any individual product from being forgotten, a hierarchical breakdown of the project product is mandatory. It is important that the breakdown comprises products (nouns) and not activities (verbs). In addition to the project products to be delivered, the breakdown should also consist of external products to be delivered by third parties and intermediate products necessary in the course of the delivery.

The product breakdown structure can be drafted in any format that is suitable for the circumstances (e.g. traditional or as a mind map). In the breakdown, the (event-driven) management products should be included as well. Producing management products costs time and money and this should not be forgotten.

Write the Product Descriptions

A Product Description has to be produced for all identified products in the product breakdown. Although it is not required for external products, preparing a Product Description is recommended.

A Product Description must be prepared as soon as an individual product is identified. A Product Description has to be baselined as soon as the Stage Plan for the stage in which the product is to be produced has been approved. A Product Description is often the first document included in the Configuration Item Record. Furthermore, each change to the Product Description immediately requires an adjustment to the Configuration Item Record.

Create the product flow diagram

As a foundation for the final planning, it is necessary to know in what order the products are to be produced and used. To this end, a product flow diagram is prepared as a final step in the focus on the product. In this flow diagram, all products from the product breakdown structure are scheduled sequentially.

During preparation of the product flow diagram, new products are frequently identified for the plan. These products have to be added to the product breakdown structure in order to be certain that both diagrams continue to match one another. Product Descriptions also have to be prepared for these 'forgotten' products.

When preparing a product flow diagram, it is advisable to fill in the flow diagram both from the perspective of the plan's starting point (from front to back) and also from the perspective of the plan's end (from back to front). This yields the best results.

Roles and responsibilities for the Plans theme

For an overview of the roles and responsibilities for the Plans theme, see table 7.1.

Table 7.1 Roles and responsibilities for the Plans theme

Corporate / programme management	Project Manager (PM)
• Provide corporate/programme planning standards • Set project tolerances in mandate • Approve project Exception Plans	• Develop Project and Stage Plans • Design management and technical stages • Instruct corrective actions when Work Package tolerances are forecasted to exceed • Prepare stage and project Exception Plans
Executive • Approves Project Plan • Defines stage tolerances • Approves Stage and Exception Plans • Commits business resources to Stage Plans	**Team Manager (TM)** • Prepare and update Team Plans • Prepare schedules for each Work Package • Escalate to PM when Work Package tolerances are forecasted to exceed
Senior User • Ensures Project and Stage Plans remain consistent from user perspective • Commits user resources to Stage Plans	**Project Assurance** • Monitor changes to the Project Plan on impact to the Business Case • Monitor stage and project progress against agreed tolerances
Senior Supplier • Ensures Project and Stage Plans remain consistent from supplier perspective • Commits supplier resources to Stage Plan	**Project Support** • Assist with compilation of plans • Contribute with specialist expertise • Baseline and store plans

Multiple choice - Plans theme

PL01. What is the purpose of the Plans theme?
a. To facilitate the implementation, communication and control of the output by defining the means of delivering the products
b. To ensure alignment of PRINCE2 with the planning tool that is used
c. To support the senior management by defining the project end date
d. To establish the basis by which to monitor and compare actual achievements against those planned.

PL02. How is the manage by exception principle supported by the Plans theme?
a. By defining the purpose, quality criteria, method and responsibilities for each of the project's products
b. By defining and capturing the respective targets and tolerances
c. By defining separate Project and Stage Plans
d. By capturing stages in the Project Plan

PL03. Which are the levels of plans recommended by PRINCE2?
1. Project Plan
2. Master Plan
3. Stage Plan
4. Team Plan
   a. 1, 2, 3
   b. 1, 2, 4
   c. 1, 3, 4
   d. 2, 3, 4

PL04. Identify the missing words in the following sentence.
The [?] is prepared at the end of the starting up stage
a. Initiation Stage Plan
b. Exception Plan
c. Stage Plan
d. Project Plan

PL05. The replacement of the Project Plan by an Exception Plan must be approved by?
A. Executive
B. The Project Board
C. The Project Assurance
D. The corporate or programme management

PL06. Identify the missing words in the following sentence.
Based on [?] the product breakdown structure can be drafted
a. The Project Product Description
b. The product flow diagram
c. Product descriptions
d. Product specifications

PL07. Which of the following statements is NOT correct?
a. All Product Descriptions must be prepared at the initiation stage as part of the Project Plan
b. The Product Description has to be baselined as soon as the Stage Plan for the stage in which the product is to be produced has been approved
c. A Product Description has to be produced for all identified products in the product breakdown
d. For each approved change request the respective Product Description has to be updated

PL08. What is NOT a responsibility of the Project Manager within the Plans theme?
a. Design technical stages
b. Define stage tolerances
c. Prepare stage and project Exception Plans
d. Develop the Project Plan

8 Risk

Purpose (RK04)

The purpose of the Risk theme is to identify, assess and control uncertainties, thereby improving the capacity of a project to be successful.

Learning outcomes

Syllabus area	Topic	Topic description	Level
Know facts, terms and concepts relating to the Risk theme. Specifically to recall:			
RK	01	The definition of a risk and the difference between a threat and an opportunity	1
RK	02	The recommended risk response types and whether they are used to respond to a threat or an opportunity	1
RK	03	The difference between a risk owner and a risk actionee	1
Understand how the Risk theme relates to the principles; the approach to the treatment of this theme; how it is applied throughout the project lifecycle and the responsibilities involved. Specifically to identify:			
RK	04	The purpose of the Risk theme	2
RK	05	The steps within the recommended risk management procedure	2
RK	06	The purpose of a risk budget	2
RK	07	The risk probability, risk impact and risk proximity	2
RK	08	The difference between cause, event and effect when expressing a risk	2
RK	09	The purpose of a Risk Management Strategy and a Risk Register	2
RK	10	The concept of risk appetite and risk tolerance	2

Definitions

- **Risk** – Uncertain event or set of events that, should it occur, will have an effect on the achievement of objectives.
- **Threat** – An uncertain event that could have a negative impact on objectives.
- **Opportunity** – An uncertain event that could have a positive impact on objectives.

Introduction

Every project has its risks. Risks cannot be avoided. Due to the temporary nature of a project and the large number of stakeholders often involved, projects attract a higher degree of risk than the activities involved in day-to-day operations. Projects yield results necessary to implement change and achieve new benefits. These results are commonly surrounded by uncertainties. These uncertainties will not always have a direct impact on the project output to be delivered, but they do have a direct impact on the business justification for the project. From this perspective, these 'business risks' also have to be included in the project management.

Risk can occur during the whole lifecycle of the project. Therefore risk management should not be an incidental action at the start of the project, but rather an integral aspect of managing projects throughout their life span.

Relations to the principles

The Risk theme supports the continued business justification principle through the proactive identification, assessment and control of risks that might affect the delivery of the project's objectives.

PRINCE2 approach to the Risk theme

Management of risk is based on a number of risk management principles, such as understanding the project's context, involving stakeholders, defining clear roles and responsibilities, establishing a support structure and supportive culture for risk management, reviewing the risk regularly and monitoring for early warning indicators.

It is important to prepare a risk management strategy at the start of the project in the Initiating a Project process and to maintain a Risk Register. The approach to risk is dependent on the risk appetite of the organization.

The definition of a risk and the difference between a threat and an opportunity (RK01)

A risk is an uncertain event or set of events that, should it occur, will have an effect on the achievement of the objectives. Risks comprise a combination of opportunities and threats *and* the impact these opportunities and threats have on the objectives that are to be fulfilled.

Within PRINCE2, the aspects of time, money, scope, quality, risks and benefits are defined as the objectives to be fulfilled. Aspects like health, safety, security and the environment are not mentioned individually by PRINCE2, but can of course be incorporated into the project as separate objectives.

The majority of uncertain events and circumstances entail both opportunities and threats. And so it is important that opportunities and threats are managed integrally as risks.

The concept of risk appetite and risk tolerance (RK10)

Risk appetite is the attitude of an organization in relation to taking risks, which subsequently determines the degree of risk acceptance.

Risk tolerance is the threshold level of risk exposure which, if a risk crosses this threshold, necessitates that the risk is escalated to the next management level.

The purpose of a Risk Management Strategy and a Risk Register (RK09)

The purpose of the Risk Management Strategy is to record the specific risk management techniques and standards to be applied, and the responsibilities for achieving an effective risk management procedure. This strategy is developed by the Project Manager in the initiation stage and is approved as part of the Project Initiation Documentation by the Project Board during authorization of the project. The Risk Management Strategy is evaluated and (if necessary) updated, as a minimum at the end of each management stage.

The purpose of the Risk Register is to record the indentified risks relating to the project, including their status and history. It is used to capture and maintain all information about the identified threats and opportunities. The Risk Register is created in the Initiating a Project process and will be updated at any time when the status of the risks have to be updated.

Risk categories can be legal, commercial, etc. For the explanation of the other specific risk terms, see below.

The risk probability, risk impact and risk proximity (RK07)

Within the Risk Management Strategy the scales for probability, impact, and proximity of risks should be defined. The probability is the likelihood that a risk will occur. The impact is the result of a threat or opportunity if either of these occur. The proximity is the time in which risks can occur. The expected value of a risk is defined by the probability multiplied by the impact of that risk.

The steps within the recommended risk management procedure (RK05)

PRINCE2 has a risk management procedure comprising five steps (see figure 8.1).

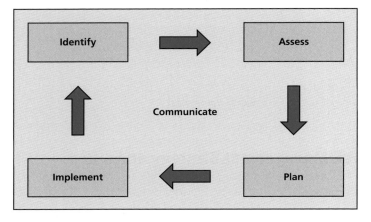

Figure 8.1 Steps within the risk management procedure

Identify

The identification of the risks can be further divided into:

- **Identifying context** – This involves gathering information about the project itself, the context and the objectives, plus the development of the Risk Management Strategy.
- **Identifying risks** – This involves identifying and recording the individual risks, identifying possible warning indicators and understanding the vision of stakeholders with regard to the risks identified.

Assess

Assessing the risks can be further divided into:

- **Estimating** – Estimating the probability, impact and proximity for each individual risk and how the impact of the threats and opportunities may change over time. The risk owner should be established for each individual risk.
- **Evaluating** – Reviewing the net effect of the aggregation of all the risks for the project. This makes it possible to assess whether the aggregated risk level still falls within the risk tolerance for the project as a whole and, thus, whether there is still a business justification to implement or continue the project (as the case may be). It also enables decisions to be taken on when risk responses should or should not be taken.

Plan

This involves preparing specific management responses to the threats and opportunities that have been defined. In this step it is advisable to determine several responses to the individual threats and opportunities, and evaluate the effectiveness thereafter, and not simply limit the response to the first solution that comes to mind. This is particularly important as the final decision about the risk responses has to be made by higher management. To support the identification of the appropriate risk responses, several types of responses are categorized (see figure 8.1). After approval by the appropriate management level, the approved risk responses will be incorporated in the respective plans.

Implement

In order to implement the risk response it must be established that risk owners have been appointed for all of the individual risks. Look at whether the agreed risk responses are being implemented. Check whether the risk responses are effective, the risks are actually removed or reduced, and the opportunities are actually enhanced or ensured. Take corrective action if the anticipated effect is not forthcoming.

If, after implementing the agreed risk responses, the residual risk is higher than the risk tolerance agreed, the risk will have to be escalated once again and additional risk responses will be required.

Communicate

For the effective management of risks it is necessary to have frequent communication on any new risks identified and the status of known risks. A risk analysis should not only be performed during the start-up stage and the initiation stage but each time a plan is prepared or updated, each time the Business Case is updated and each time the impact of an issue is considered. Risk management is a continuous process throughout the project.

Communicating on risks must be done in every report and during every meeting. Risks are communicated as part of the Checkpoint and Highlight Reports and as part of the End Stage and End Project Reports.

The Team Manager must escalate new opportunities and threats to the Project Manager by means of an issue.

If at the stage level the risks threaten to exceed the risk tolerance, then the Project Manager will have to escalate this to the Project Board using an Exception Report with proposals for new risk responses. If at the project level there is a possibility of the risk tolerance being exceeded, then the Executive will have to escalate this to the corporate or programme management.

During the Project Board meetings, the most significant risks *and* the aggregate risk level for the entire project will remain a subject for discussion when reviewing the continued viability of the project.

Finally, the application and effectiveness of risk management will have to be evaluated regularly. This should be done at least at the end of each management stage and at the end of the project. Points for improvement are to be included in the Lessons Log and in the Lessons Report.

The difference between cause, event and effect when expressing a risk (RK08)

It is important for the identification of risks that they are recorded in an unambiguous way. It obviously makes a difference if a risk will cause a rejection of a batch or jeopardize the continuation of the entire organization. It is therefore strongly recommended that risks are identified on the basis of a defined risk cause and the possible risk effect: a risk is that ...<event/condition>... as a result of which ...<result>... with the effect of ...<consequence>... (see figure 8.2).

Figure 8.2 Risk cause, event and effect

The risk cause is the risk driver. The risk event is the threat or opportunity. The risk effect is the impact on the objectives of the project.

The recommended risk response types and whether they are used to respond to a threat or an opportunity (RK02)

Within the planning step of risk management, the risk responses are identified. Here a distinction has to be made between threat and opportunity responses (see table 8.1).

* **Avoid** – Typically involves a change of approach to ascertain that the threat no longer exists or no longer has an impact.
* **Reduce** – Selecting a response that will reduce the probability, the impact or both.
* **Fallback** – A special form of reduction; planning a response that is not deployed until the risk actually occurs or (as the case may be) threatens to occur. The probability remains the same, but the impact decreases.
* **Transfer** – A special form of reduction; the negative financial effect of the risk is transferred to someone else.
* **Share** – The opportunities and threats are shared with a third party.
* **Accept** – A deliberate decision is taken not to implement any risk responses to a threat on the assumption that taking action will not be effective until the threat actually occurs.
* **Exploit** – Ensuring that the opportunity is seized and that the impact will be realized.
* **Enhance** – Enhancing the probability and/or positive effect of the opportunity.
* **Reject** – A deliberate decision not to implement any responses on the assumption that taking action will not be effective until the opportunity actually occurs.

For risks that are below the risk tolerance limit, the Project Manager can decide on the appropriate risk responses. Risks above the risk tolerance limit have to be escalated to the Project Board. After a decision has been made, the agreed actions must be incorporated into the plans in question. Often a combination of risk responses is implemented for several risks simultaneously.

Table 8.1 Risk responses (based on OGC PRINCE2 material)

Effect	Threat Responses	Opportunity Responses
High	Avoid	Exploit
↑↓	Reduce Fallback Transfer	Enhance
	Share	
Low	Accept	Reject

The difference between a risk owner and a risk actionee (RK03)

A risk owner is the person responsible for managing, monitoring and controlling all aspects of a specific risk, including implementation of the risk responses. In respect of the risk, the risk owner reports to the Project Manager.

If the implementation of a risk response does not fall within a risk owner's remit, then a separate risk actionee will have to be appointed. A risk actionee is the person responsible for implementing a specific risk response, without being responsible for the other aspects of a particular risk. The risk actionee reports on the implementation to the relevant risk owner or owners (as the case may be).

The purpose of a risk budget (RK06)

A risk budget is a budget to finance costs relating to risk responses *and* the possible costs of the impact of the risks, should they materialize. When estimating the possible costs of the impact of the risks in total, it is best to use the aggregate expected financial value of all risks. For those risks that have not yet been foreseen it is recommended to include a contingency sum.

Roles and responsibilities for the Risk theme

For an overview of the roles and responsibilities for the Risk theme, see table 8.2.

Table 8.2 Roles and responsibilities for the Risk theme

Corporate / programme management	Project Manager (PM)
• Provide risk management policy • Provide risk management process guide	• Create Risk Management Strategy • Create and maintain Risk Register • Responsible for management of risks
Executive • Accountable for risk management (strategy) • Responsible for business risks • Escalate risk to corporate or programme management	**Team Manager (TM)** • Participate in identifying, assessing and controlling risks
Project Board • Inform PM about external risks • Decision taking on risks	**Project Assurance** • Review risk management practices • Ensure alignment with strategy
Senior User • Ensure user aspects of risks are managed	**Project Support** • Assist PM in maintaining Risk Register
Senior Supplier • Ensure supplier aspects of risks are managed	**Risk owner** • Management of individual risk
	Risk actionee • Carry out risk response action

Multiple choice - Risk theme

RK01. What is a purpose of the Risk Management theme?
a. Identify, assess and control uncertainties
b. Select a response that will reduce the probability, the impact or both
c. Review the net effect of the aggregation of all risks for the project
d. Establish mechanisms to monitor and compare achievements against plans

RK02. How does the Risk theme support the continued business justification principle?
a. By the proactive identification, assessment and control of risks that might affect the delivery of the project's objectives
b. By capturing and maintaining all information about the identified threats and opportunities
c. By checking whether the risk responses are effective and the risks are actually removed
d. By ensuring that the opportunity is seized and that the impact will be realized

RK03. Which statement correctly defines an opportunity?
a. An uncertain event that could have an impact on objectives
b. An uncertain event or set of events that, should it occur, will have an effect on the achievement of objectives
c. An uncertain event that could have a positive impact on objectives
d. A positive event that has already occurred

RK04. The concept of risk appetite is:
a. Not a concept used by PRINCE2
b. Only applicable for IT-projects
c. The attitude of an organization with regard to taking risk
d. The threshold level of risk exposure which, if a risk crosses this threshold, necessitates that the risk is escalated

RK05. What is the purpose of the Risk Management Strategy?
a. To record the identified risks relating to the project, including their status and history
b. To describe the specific risk management techniques and standards to be applied and the responsibilities for achieving an effective risk management procedure
c. To record all risks relating to the project, including their history
d. To record all risks that the Project Manager is responsible for, including their status and history

RK06. Which of the following is the best definition for probability?
a. The likelihood of success
b. The frequency of the risk occurrence
c. The likelihood of a risk occurring
d. The likelihood of a loss

RK07. What are the steps within the risk management procedure?
1. Assess
2. Plan
3. Review
4. Communicate
    a. 1, 2, 3
    b. 1, 2, 4
    c. 1, 3, 4
    d. 2, 3, 4

RK08. Identify the missing words in the following sentence.
A risk cause is [?]
a. An impact on the objectives of the organization
b. A threat or opportunity
c. An impact on the objectives of the project
d. A risk driver

RK09. Which of the following risk response types are used to respond to a threat?
1. Avoid
2. Reduce
3. Reject
4. Fallback
    a. 1, 2, 3
    b. 1, 2, 4
    c. 1, 3, 4
    d. 2, 3, 4

RK10. Identify the missing words in the following sentence.
A [?] is responsible for implementing a specific risk response, without being responsible for the other aspects of that particular risk.
a. Risk owner
b. Project Board
c. Risk actionee
d. Risk Register

RK11. Identify the missing words in the following sentence.
A risk budget is a budget to finance costs related to risk responses and [?]
a. 4 % of related operational risks
b. The costs of the management of risks
c. The possible costs of the impact, as the risks occur
d. The costs for the implementation of the risk strategy

RK12. Which of the following is NOT a responsibility of the Executive within the Risk theme?
a. Ensure alignment with corporate strategy
b. Provide risk management policy
c. Responsible for business risks
d. Escalate risk to corporate or programme

9 Change

Purpose (CH03)

The purpose of the Change theme is to identify, assess and control any potential and approved change to the baseline.

Learning outcomes

Syllabus area	Topic	Topic description	Level
Know facts, terms and concepts relating to the Change theme. Specifically to recall the:			
CH	01	Three types of issue	1
CH	02	Five typical activities of a configuration management procedure	1
Understand how the Change theme relates to the principles; the approach to the treatment of this theme; how it is applied throughout the project lifecycle and the responsibilities involved. Specifically to identify:			
CH	03	The purpose of the Change theme	2
CH	04	The purpose of a change budget	2
CH	05	The purpose of a: • Configuration Management Strategy; • Configuration Item Record; • Issue Report; • Issue Register; • Product Status Account.	2
CH	06	The steps in the recommended issue and change control procedure	2

Definitions

- **Issue** – Relevant unplanned event that has occurred and requires attention to resolve or conclude.
- **Request for change** – Request to change the baseline of a product, process or condition.
- **Off-specification** – Project product that (as expected) does not comply with the specifications or has not been/is not being delivered.
- **Problem/concern** – Issue that is not a request for change or an exception to the specification and that the Project Manager needs to resolve or escalate.
- **Baseline** – Recorded or approved status of a product or item that, once it occurs, is subject to change control.

Introduction

The customer's needs change. Suppliers suggest improvements. In a project, change is inevitable as the project implements change to the environment itself. Therefore, to control the project, the change to the project has to be managed. For the important assets of a project, the management of the project needs to know the actual status of the products and if the work conforms with the approved baselines.

In addition to changes to the products, issues can be raised due to a non-conformance with the specifications or as a result of any other problems or concerns that are brought to the attention of the management. All issues have to be managed in order to control the project and to deliver the project product successfully. Issues may be raised by anyone during the project at any time.

The aim of issue and change control is, therefore, not to prevent change happening or issues arising, but rather to identify issues and (proposed) changes and have them assessed and managed. You cannot prevent issues; at most you can negate them.

Effective issue and change control is necessary to:
• Prevent scope creep;
• Be able to manage the effect of issues and changes on the rest of the project;
• Ascertain the effect on the desirability, achievability and viability of the project;
• Ensure acceptance by stakeholders.

Relations to the principles

The Change theme supports the manage by exception principle, by ensuring that issues possibly affecting the project's performance targets are appropriately managed.

Three types of issues (CH01)

Three types of issues can be distinguished:
• **Request for change** – A proposal for a change to the baseline of a product, process or status.
• **Off-specification** – A product that does not satisfy, or that obviously will not satisfy, the agreed specifications.
• **Problem or a concern** – Any other issue that has to be resolved or has to be escalated by the Project Manager.

PRINCE2 approach to change

To ensure that a project is successful, we have to manage the assets of the project.

Configuration management is the technical and administrative activity concerned with the creation, maintenance and controlled change of the configuration throughout the life of a product.

All deliverables or products within a project need to be controlled. Configuration management is used to provide that control. A configuration item is an entity that is subject to configuration management. The configuration of a project is the aggregate of all the products to be delivered in a project, also called the project product.

Configuration management encompasses identification, maintenance, control of the change, status justification and verification of the configuration items. Change management is, therefore, part of configuration management.

The purpose of configuration management is to ensure that:
• Everyone always works with the right products;
• All products are easily traceable;
• The actual status of the various products is always known;
• These products are not changed without authorization.

Within PRINCE2 the following management products are used to manage the assets of the project:
• Configuration Management Strategy;
• Configuration Item Records;
• Product Status Account;
• Issue Register and Issue Reports.

Configuration management can be used for specialist products as well for management products.

Purpose of the configuration management products (CH05)

The Configuration Management Strategy – describes how and by whom the products in a project will be controlled and protected. The Configuration Management Strategy must be derived from the corporate or programme organization's configuration management policy and configuration management processes, and will be prepared in the Initiating a Project process and reviewed at the stage and project end.

A Configuration Item Record – is a record in which all aspects of a configuration item to be controlled are set down, such as the status of the progress, version and variants of a configuration item, and the interrelations with other configuration items. Every time the status or one of the other aspects of a configuration item changes, the relevant Configuration Item Record has to be updated. The individual Configuration Item Record is created when the respective Stage or Project Plan is prepared.

A Product Status Account – is a report that provides information about the status of the configuration items. The status list can cover the entire project, a stage, or just a Work Package. A Product Status Account is primarily used by the Project Manager to check the status and the version numbers of the configuration items. Such a Product Status Account is often prepared for the purpose of assessing a stage's status as part of the Managing a Stage Boundary process and during preparations for closing the project.

An Issue Register – is a report in which all issues are recorded and which have to be formally monitored and acted on, and in which the status of these issues is kept up-to-date. The Issue Register is created by Project Support at the same time as the Configuration Management Strategy is being prepared by the Project Manager. The Project Manager is responsible for recording and updating the issues in the Issue Register. Formal issues originally entered in the Daily Log should be transferred to the Issue Register once the Issue Register is created.

The Issue Report – is a record containing all information pertaining to an issue that must be acted on formally. In the Issue Report the issue is described in more detail than in the Issue Register. The Issue Report is prepared during the capturing and reviewing issues and risks activity in the Controlling a Stage process. The Project Manager is responsible for preparing and updating the Issue Report.

The priority describes how urgently an issue has to be dealt with. The severity indicates the possible level of impact of the issue on the project and, with that, it determines the level of management that is required to take a decision on this matter. Both should be given in terms of a defined scale.

The initial Issue Register is created during Initiating a Project and updated during the project. The Issue Report is created for each issue recorded in the Issue Register.

The purpose of a change budget (CH04)

It is the responsibility of the Project Board to assess change requests and off-specifications and make appropriate decisions on these. This can take up a lot of time; it often requires a considerable degree of knowledge and insight into the situation and has to be considered in-depth with other parties outside the project in order to come up with the correct decision. In view of the principle of managing by exception, it is therefore often desirable to delegate the authority for making such decisions to a Change Authority, who can make these decisions on behalf of the Project Board.

Small changes and slight off-specifications can even be left to the Project Manager. For more important decisions, the authority can be delegated to a separate Change Authority, with critical changes and off-specifications always having to be passed back to the Project Board. If changes and off-specifications are forecasted to exceed the agreed stage tolerances, these changes and off-specifications should always be escalated to the Project Board.

In order to operate effectively, it is preferable to give a Change Authority its own budget. The benefit of this budget is that costs relating to changes do not have to be at the expense of the operational budget, or that the Executive does not have to ask for extra budget from the corporate or programme management.

A separate Change Authority combined with a change budget and a good prioritization of changes (e.g. MoSCoW) can prevent a torrent of changes.

Five typical activities of a configuration management procedure (CH02)

Configuration management consists of five typical activities:

- **Planning** – Decide upon the required level of configuration management:
  - Which products should come under configuration management;
  - The level of detail to be recorded;
  - Agree on how configuration management is to be put into practice.
- **Identification** – Identify and record the individual configuration items.
- **Control** – 'Freeze' the approved baselines. Release products and the respective information to authorized parties only. Adopt authorized changes in new versions. Archive the old versions.
- **Status accounting** – Record and report on the current and historical status of configuration items and the changes that have been implemented.
- **Verification** – Guarantee that the current status of all configuration items corresponds to the official status recorded in the Configuration Item Records. The Project Support has to check regularly that the correct configuration items are being used on the shop floor and that the Configuration Item Records are up-to-date, especially at stage ends and at the project end (when they may be subject to audits).

The steps in the recommended issue and change control procedure (CH06)

The recommended issue and change control procedure has five stages (see figure 9.1).

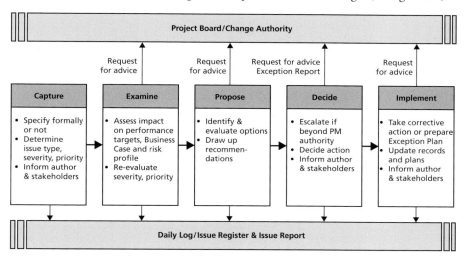

Figure 9.1 Issue and change control procedure (based on OGC PRINCE2 material)

- **Capture** – Specify whether an issue can be dealt with informally or not. Specify the type of issue and an initial indication of the severity and priority of the issue. Record the issue in the Daily Log or in the Issue Register. For the latter, an Issue Report should also be produced. Inform the person who reported the issue that it has been recorded. Inform the stakeholders involved, in line with the agreements in the Communication Management Strategy.
- **Examine** – Investigate what the impact of the issue is on the stage and project objectives, the Business Case, the risk profile and on the interests of the individual stakeholders. Re-evaluate the severity and priority of the issue. Update the Issue Report and the status in the Issue Register.
- **Propose** – Identify and evaluate the possible measures. Draw up a recommendation. Record the possible corrective action and the recommendation in the Issue Report. Update the status in the Issue Register.
- **Decide** – Present the issues to the person authorized to decide on them. Ensure that the necessary decisions are made. Record the decisions made in the Issue Report. Update the Issue Register. Inform the person who reported the issue and the stakeholders concerned.
- **Implement** – Implement the agreed measures or prepare an Exception Plan, by order of the Project Board. Close the issue as soon as the measures have been implemented. If the measures implemented do not lead to the desired effect, record this as a new issue or re-open the existing issue. Inform the person who reported the issue and the stakeholders concerned.

A Project Board (or a Change Authority) can approve or reject a change request, but can also postpone the decision, request further information, or request that an Exception Plan be produced. With regard to an off-specification, the Project Board (or a Change Authority) actually has the same options, even though they may talk of accepting an exception to a specification rather than approving it. A concession is an off-specification accepted by a Change Authority or Project Board without corrective action.

Roles and responsibilities for the Change theme

For an overview of the roles and responsibilities for the Change theme, see table 9.1.

Table 9.1 Roles and responsibilities for the Change theme

Corporate / programme management	Project Manager (PM)
• Provide corporate/programme Configuration Management Strategy **Executive** • Approve Configuration Management Strategy • Set scales for severity and priority • Determine change authority/budget • Respond to request for advice • Take decisions on escalated issues **Senior User/ Supplier** • Respond to request for advice • Take decisions on escalated Issues **Change Authority** • Take decisions on requests for change and off-specifications • Refer to Project Board if delegated authority or allocated change budget are forecast to be exceeded • CM = Configuration Management • CC = Change Control	• Prepare Configuration Management Strategy • Manage CM & CC procedures, assisted by Project Support • Create and maintain Issue Register, assisted by Project Support • Ensure TMs implement CM & CC measures • Implement corrective actions **Team Manager (TM)** • Implement CM & CC measures • Implement corrective actions **Project Assurance** • Advice on establishing CM Strategy • Advice on examining and solving issues **Project Support** • Maintain Configuration Item Records • Assist the PM to maintain the Issue Register • Assist the PM with CM & CC procedures • Produce Product Status Accounts

Multiple choice - Change theme

CH01. What is the purpose of the Change theme?
a. Identify, assess and control any potential and approved change to the baseline
b. Ensure stakeholder acceptance
c. Manage the effect of issues and changes
d. Prevent scope creep

CH02. Identify the missing words in the following sentence.
The Change theme supports the [?] principle by ensuring that issues possibly affecting the project's performance targets are appropriately managed.
a. Manage by exception
b. Learn from experience
c. Manage by stages
d. Focus on products

CH03. What are the three types of issue?
1. Outside-specification
2. Request for change
3. Off-specification
4. Problem/concern
    a. 1, 2, 3
    b. 1, 2, 4
    c. 1, 3, 4
    d. 2, 3, 4

CH04. Which of the following is NOT a purpose of configuration management?
a. Ensure that everyone always works with the right products
b. Act as a document filing system for all project documents
c. The actual status of the various products is always known
d. Ensure that products are not changed without authorization

CH05. What is covered by the activity status accounting within configuration management?
a. Record the current status of a configuration item
b. Check regularly that the current configuration items are used
c. Archive old versions
d. Define the level of detail to be recorded

CH06. What is the purpose of a Product Status Account?
a. Provides information about the status of all products
b. Describes how and by whom the products in a project will be controlled and protected
c. An account in which all aspects of a configuration item to be controlled are recorded
d. Provides information about the status of the configuration items

CH07. Identify the missing words in the following sentence.

In order to manage changes effectively, it is preferable to give a [?] their own budget.

a. Change Advisory Board

b. Change Authority

c. Project Assurance

d. Team Manager

CH08 Which of the following is NOT a correct description of a baseline?

a. A reference level against which an entity is monitored and controlled

b. A snapshot of a release or product frozen at a point in time for a particular purpose

c. A product that needs to be updated during the course of the project

d. A product that may only be changed with the agreement of the appropriate authorities

CH09. Which of the following is NOT a step in the recommended issue and change control procedure?

a. Capture

b. Examine

c. Suggest

d. Decide

CH10. Which of the following is NOT a responsibility of Project Support within the Change theme?

a. Maintain Configuration Item Records

b. Produce Product Status Accounts

c. Maintain the Issue Register

d. Administer changes

10 Progress

Purpose (PG03)

The purpose of the Progress theme is to establish mechanisms in order to be able to monitor and compare actual achievements against those planned. This is so that a forecast can be provided on the project objectives to be fulfilled, including the continued viability of the project, and to enable any unacceptable deviations to be controlled.

Learning outcomes

Syllabus area	Topic	Topic description	Level
Know facts, terms and concepts relating to the Progress theme. Specifically to recall the:			
PG	01	Lines of authority and reporting between the four levels of management	1
Understand how the Progress theme relates to the principles; the approach to the treatment of this theme; how it is applied throughout the project lifecycle and the responsibilities involved. Specifically to identify:			
PG	02	The difference between event-driven and time-driven controls	2
PG	03	The purpose of the Progress theme	2
PG	04	The concept of management stages and the difference between management and technical stages	2
PG	05	The factors to consider in identifying management stages	2
PG	06	Tolerance(s): when and how tolerances are set and exceptions reported, in which management products tolerances are documented, and how management by exception applies to the different levels of management	2
PG	07	The purpose of the Daily Log, the Lessons Log and the Work Package	2
PG	08	The purpose of the End Stage Report, the End Project Report and the Lessons Report	2
PG	09	The purpose of the Checkpoint Report, the Highlight Report and the Exception Report	2

Definitions

- **Progress** – The measure of the achievement of the objectives of a plan.
- **Exception** – A situation in which it can be expected that the agreed tolerance levels of a plan will be exceeded.
- **Tolerance** – The permissible deviation above and below a plan's target.
- **(Progress) controls** – Management products and procedures to monitor progress against the allowed tolerances and to report the progress to the next management levels for information and decision-making.

Introduction

The periodic monitoring and controlling of progress is one of the critical success factors in managing a project. It is not only important to produce a plan, have it approved and then react to all issues that are raised. It is also important to reflect periodically on the achievements and the amount of effort still required to deliver the project output. This provides the input needed to look forward and to adjust the course of the project proactively.

Relations to the principles

The Progress theme contributes directly to the principle of managing by stages, by providing the Project Board with the opportunity to assess the viability of the project on decision points and to ensure control of the project.

The Progress theme contributes directly to the principle of managing by exception by:
- Setting tolerances for the project objectives to establish limits of delegated authority;
- Providing a mechanism to monitor progress against the tolerances;
- Escalating to the next management level in cases where one or more tolerances are forecasted to exceed the tolerances.

The Progress theme contributes directly to the principles of learning from experience, as lessons are included in the management reports so actions can be taken to improve the performance.

PRINCE2 approach

In a PRINCE2 project, progress is controlled by:
- Delegating responsibilities *and* authority;
- Dividing the project into management stages;
- Time-driven and event-driven reports and reviews;
- Raising exceptions.

A summary of the project level controls is documented in the Project Initiation Documentation.

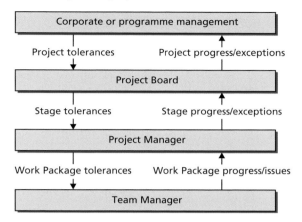

Figure 10.1 The four levels of management (source: Managing Successful Projects with PRINCE2, produced by OGC)

Lines of authority and reporting between the four levels of management (PG01)

Between each of the four management levels in the project management structure, agreements have to be made on responsibilities and authority to delegate, and these are documented in the various tolerances. In addition, each management level has to report regularly back to the next higher management level on the progress against the allowed tolerances (see figure 10.1).

Tolerance(s) (PG06)

PRINCE2 recognizes six tolerance areas that have to be managed, namely time, money, scope, quality, risks and benefits. The various tolerances are recorded at project, stage and Work Package level in different management products (see table 10.1).

Table 10.1 Tolerance areas for each level (source: Managing Successful Projects with PRINCE2, produced by OGC)

Tolerance areas	Project level tolerances	Stage level tolerances	Work Package level tolerances	Product level tolerances
Time	Project Plan	Stage Plan	Work Package	NA
Cost	Project Plan	Stage Plan	Work Package	NA
Scope	Project Plan	Stage Plan	Work Package	NA
Risk	Risk Management Strategy	Stage Plan	Work Package	NA
Quality	Project Product Description	NA	NA	Product Description
Benefits	Business Case	NA	NA	NA

- **Time, money and scope tolerances** – Recorded in the Project Plan and in the relevant Stage Plans and Work Packages.
- **Risk tolerances** – Recorded at project level in the Risk Management Strategy. At the stage and Work Package level the risk tolerances are recorded in the relevant Stage Plans and Work Packages.
- **Quality tolerances** – Recorded at project level in the Project Product Description. At the stage and Work Package level, quality tolerances are recorded in the relevant Product Descriptions.
- **Benefit tolerances** – In PRINCE2 these are only recorded at project level in the Business Case.

Time and money are the primary tolerance areas. From the perspective of PRINCE2, the tolerances in quality must be handled with the utmost care.

If it is anticipated that the agreed tolerances will be exceeded, an exception must be escalated to the next higher level of management:

- **Exception to Work Package tolerances** – If it is anticipated that a Work Package tolerance will be exceeded, then the Team Manager must escalate this to the Project Manager by means of an issue. If the risk of exceeding a Work Package tolerance stays within the stage tolerance, then the Project Manager must take corrective action and authorize one or more new or adapted Work Packages for the relevant Team Managers.
- **Exception to stage tolerances** – If it is anticipated that a stage tolerance will be exceeded, the Project Manager must escalate this to the Project Board using an Exception Report. The Project Board can decide simply to go ahead with the project, or can ask for an Exception Plan. If in doubt, the Project Board can ask for further information and/or can ask for advice from the corporate or programme management.
- **Exception to project tolerances** – If it is anticipated that a project tolerance will be exceeded, then the Project Manager must also escalate this to the Project Board using an Exception Report, but the Project Board itself must escalate this further to the corporate or programme management for a decision. In consultation with the corporate or programme management, the Project Board can decide to go ahead with the project, request an Exception Plan, or decide to end the project prematurely.

The concept of management stages and the difference between management and technical stages (PG04)

It does not make sense to schedule a meeting with the complete Project Board for all individual milestones of the project. The concept of management stages provides the Project Board with the opportunity to assess the viability of the project and to ensure the control of progress on predefined decision points during the delivery of the project only. In this way it supports the principle of management by exception.

In this, it is important to distinguish the differences between management and technical stages:

Management stages – Comprise temporary divisions in time, linked to go/no go decisions pertaining to continuation of the project. There are at least two management stages in every project - the initiation stage and the delivery stage. The delivery stage can be further divided into several individual management stages, depending on the complexity and the context of the project.

Technical stages – Are characterized by the application of a set of techniques or specialist work. Technical stages often include design stage, production stage and roll-out stage. Technical stages can overlap with one another. There are usually more technical stages than management stages.

The management and technical stages are defined in the Initiating a Project process and captured in the Project Plan.

The factors to consider in identifying management stages (PG05)

The **number** of management stages depends on:
- How far in advance plans can be reasonably made;
- Where the decision points are in the project;
- The level of risks within the project;
- The desired extent of project control; too many short stages as opposed to too few long stages;
- Confidence of Project Board and Project Manager that the project will be continued.

A large number of short stages offer a lot of control, but also take a significant amount of time and constantly cause interruptions to the implementation. A limited number of long stages, on the other hand, result in a lower level of control. It is possible that the project continues unnoticed, whereas in actual fact the business justification of the project in its present form may have long since disappeared.

The **length** of the management stages depends on:
- The planning horizon in which plans can still be made with sufficient accuracy;
- The technical stages in the project;
- Harmony with the corporate or programme activities;
- The overall risk level in the project.

If a go/no go decision has to be made during a technical stage, then that technical stage will have to be split up so that the first part of the stage can be delivered prior to the go/no go decision (see figure 10.2).

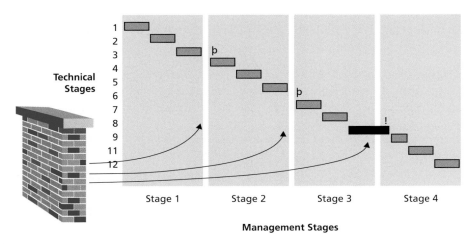

Figure 10.2 Management stages versus technical stages

Event-driven and time-driven controls (PG02)

PRINCE2 recognizes time-driven and event-driven progress controls:
- **Time-driven** – These are applied at a set point in time, or in a fixed time-based cycle, such as the Checkpoint Reports and Highlight Reports.
- **Event-driven** – These are applied when a specific event occurs, e.g. at the end of a stage (End Stage Report), at the end of a project (End Project Report), or if there is a risk of tolerances being exceeded (Exception Report).

The purpose of documents within the Progress theme: (PG07-09)

Daily Log – This is the Project Manager's project diary. It is used to record informal issues, minutes and actions that are not covered by other registers or logs. It is also used as a repository for issues and risks during the Starting up a Project process.

Lessons Log – To record lessons from previous projects that could be used in the project at hand and to record the lessons in one's own project during implementation of the project itself.

Work Package – A set of information about one or more required products that are to be delivered. The Project Manager prepares it to enable responsibility for work to be handed over to a Team Manager or a team member. In a Work Package the tolerances and reporting arrangements are defined too.

Checkpoint Report – Prepared by the individual Team Managers at agreed times, or at agreed intervals, in order to inform the Project Manager of the agreed Work Packages' progress and the issues and risks that have arisen in this regard.

Highlight Report – Prepared by the Project Manager at agreed times, or agreed intervals, in order to inform the Project Board of the highlights of the stage's progress and the issues and risks that have arisen. Highlight Reports can also be sent to other stakeholders if this has been agreed in the Communication Management Strategy.

End Stage Report – Used to give an overview of the progress and the overall situation to date at the end of a management stage. It provides the information needed by the Project Board to decide if and how to continue with the project.

Exception Report – An Exception Report is prepared by the Project Manager if the tolerances of a Project Plan or Stage Plan are forecasted to exceed agreed levels. The Exception Report gives the Project Board an insight into the possible options and recommendations for proceeding. The Exception Report is produced during the Controlling a Stage process.

End Project Report – Used during project closure to review the performance of the project in comparison to the Project Initiation Documentation.

Lessons Report – It is used to pass on any lessons that can be usefully applied to other projects, to provoke action so that the lessons become embedded in the organization.

Roles and responsibilities for the Progress theme

For an overview of the roles and responsibilities for the Progress theme, see table 10.2.

Table 10.2 Roles and responsibilities for the Progress theme

Corporate / programme management • Provide project tolerances in mandate • Approve project Exception Plans **Executive** • Provide stage tolerances • Approve stage Exception Plans • Ensure that progress towards outcome remains consistent from a business perspective • Recommend future actions in project Exception Plans **Senior User** • Ensure that progress towards the outcome remains consistent from a user perspective **Senior Supplier** • Ensure that progress towards the outcome remains consistent from a supplier perspective **Project Assurance** • Monitor changes to the Project Plan on the impact to the Business Case • Confirm stage and project progress against agreed tolerances	**Project Manager (PM)** • Authorize Work Packages • Monitor progress against Stage Plan • Produce Highlight Reports • Produce End Stage and End Project Reports • Produce Exception Reports • Maintain project's registers and logs **Team Manager (TM)** • Agree Work Package with PM • Produce Team Plan if applicable • Inform Project Support about quality checks • Produce Checkpoint Reports • Notify PM about forecast deviation from tolerances **Project Support** • Assist with compilation of reports • Contribute with specialist expertise • Maintain Issue, Risk and Quality Registers on behalf of the PM

Multiple choice - Progress theme

PG01. What is the purpose of the Progress theme?
a. To monitor and compare actual achievements against plans
b. To tailor the method to suit the project environment
c. To delegate responsibilities and authority
d. To raise exceptions

PG02. In what respect is the learning from experience principle supported by the Progress theme?
a. By setting tolerances for the project objectives, providing a mechanism to monitor progress against the tolerances and escalating to the next management level
b. By providing the Project Board with the opportunity to assess the viability of the project on decision points and to ensure control of the project
c. By including lessons in the management reports so actions can be taken to improve the performance
d. By keeping the Lessons Log up-to-date

PG03. Which of the following does NOT represent a management level in PRINC2?
a. Team Manager
b. Project Manager
c. Project Board
d. Programme Manager

PG04. Identify the missing words in the following sentence.
When using PRINCE2 [?] are only recorded at the project level in the Business Case.
a. Tolerances in time, money and scope
b. Risk tolerances
c. Quality tolerances
d. Benefit tolerances

PG05. Which of the following statements is correct with regard to management stages?
a. Should divide the project in several phases of about the same duration
b. Comprise temporary divisions in time, linked to go/no go decisions pertaining to the continuation of the project
c. Are characterized by the application of a set of techniques or specialist work
d. For small projects only one management stage is needed

PG06. Which factors should be considered when identifying management stages?
1. Decision points in the project
2. Amount of risks within the project
3. Availability of subject matter experts to undertake one of the stages
4. Desired extent of project control
    a. 1, 2, 3
    b. 1, 2, 4
    c. 1, 3, 4
    d. 2, 3, 4

PG07. Which controls are event-driven?
1. End Stage Report
2. Checkpoint Report
3. Exception Report
4. End Project Report
    a. 1, 2, 3
    b. 1, 2, 4
    c. 1, 3, 4
    d. 2, 3, 4

PG08. What is the purpose of a Daily Log?
    a. To initially record all requests for change, off-specifications, and problems/points of concern
    b. To record informal issues, minutes and actions that are not covered by other registers or logs
    c. To record the work in progress and the issues and risks that have arisen in that regard
    d. To record the daily progress reported by the Team Managers

PG09. What is the purpose of a Lessons Report?
    a. To record the lessons from previous projects that could be used in the project at hand
    b. To record the lessons in one's own project during implementation of the project itself
    c. To record any lessons that can be usefully applied to other projects
    d. To record the performance of the project in comparison to the Project Initiation Documentation

PG10. What is the purpose of an Exception Report?
    a. To provide the Project Board with an insight into the possible options and recommendations for proceeding after an exception
    b. To provide the Project Board with the reasons for an exception, so they can decide how best to continue
    c. To provide the Project Board with the information needed to decide how to continue with the project.f
    d. To provide the Project Board with the information about the actions taken, to manage an exception that has occurred

PG11. What of the following is NOT a responsibility of the Project Manager within the Progress theme?
    a. Authorize Work Packages
    b. Produce Team Plan if applicable
    c. Produce Highlight Reports
    d. Maintain registers and logs

II   PRINCE2 Processes

Managing a project involves seven processes, namely:

- **Starting up a Project (SU)** – Is the first PRINCE2 process. It describes the activities to be carried out in order to authorize initiation by the Project Board.
- **Directing a Project (DP)** – Runs throughout the duration of the project; starts on completion of the SU process, through to the CP process. It describes the activities to be carried out by the Project Board.
- **Initiating a Project (IP)** – Describes the preparatory activities that act as the basis for carrying out the project and delivering the output.
- **Controlling a Stage (CS)** – Describes the daily management undertaken by the Project Manager during a stage.
- **Managing Product Delivery (MP)** – Describes the management activities of the Team Manager to accept, execute and deliver a Work Package.
- **Managing a Stage Boundary (SB)** – Describes the preparation work to be done by the Project Manager to facilitate the Project Board in taking a go/ no go decision.
- **Closing a Project (CP)** – Describes all the preparation work to be done by the Project Manager to facilitate the handing over of the project's products, and the subsequent project closure by the Project Board.

The processes are broken down based on the activities to be performed during the project, together with those responsible for undertaking these activities.

Each process consists of a number of activities that are/can be performed within that process. Some processes are implemented once within a project, others can be implemented several times (see figure II.1).

For complex or lengthy initiations the initiation stage can be managed by applying the processes Controlling a Stage and Managing Product Delivery.

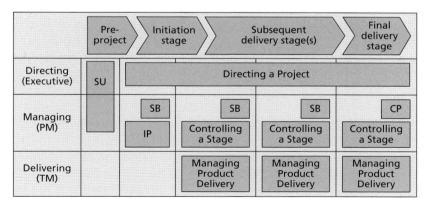

Figure II.1 PRINCE2 process model within the project lifecycle (based on OGC PRINCE2 material)

11 Starting up a Project (SU)

Purpose (SU01)

The purpose of the Starting up a Project (SU) process is to ensure that the prerequisites for initiating a project are present by answering the question 'Do we have a viable project that is worth the effort?'.

Learning outcomes

Syllabus area	Topic	Topic description	Level
Understand the SU process and how it can be applied and tailored on a project. Specifically to identify:			
SU	01	The purpose of the SU process	2
SU	02	The objectives of the SU process	2
SU	03	The context of the SU process	2
SU	04	The purpose of the Project Brief	2

Definitions

- **Project mandate** – An external product generated by an authority to commission a project, which triggers the Starting up a Project process.
- **Project approach** – A description of the manner in which the result of a project will be approached.
- **Project Brief** – A statement that describes the purpose, performance requirements and constraints of a project, in order to obtain authorization from the Project Board to start the initiation of the project.

The objectives of the SU process (SU02)

The objectives of the SU process are to ensure that:
- There is a business justification to initiate the project;
- The right authorities exist to start the project;
- There is sufficient information available to define and confirm the scope of the project;
- After evaluation, the approach for the project is selected;
- People have been appointed and the work has been planned to carry out the initiation stage;
- Time is not wasted on projects that should not start at all.

The context of the SU process (SU03)

The SU process is not part of the project but constitutes the pre-project work. A mandate, issued by the customer's corporate or programme management, is the trigger to start the SU process. This mandate should at least contain the terms of reference for the project and sufficient information to appoint the Executive and Project Manager.

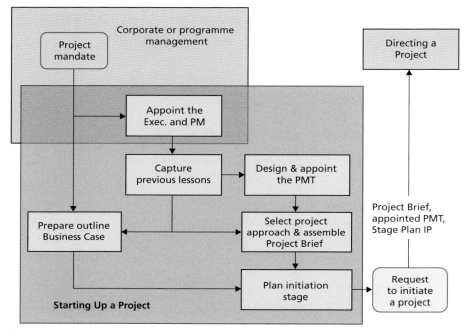

Figure 11.1 Overview of Starting up a Project process (based on OGC PRINCE2 material)

As a minimum, a project requires an Executive and a Project Manager who have agreed to implement the project. Further, the other members of the Project Board should also be appointed.

As part of the SU process the mandate is refined into the Project Brief and the work for the initiation stage is planned. It is important that there is a realistic picture of the scope, planning, acceptance criteria and prerequisites. If it is unclear at the beginning of the initiation stage what the Executive is hoping to achieve with the project, then parties will work on the project from different angles during this stage. Regular interaction is required between Project Manager and Project Board to undertake this work.

The people must have been appointed and a plan must be prepared for the work to be carried out in the next (initiation) stage, where users and suppliers are already involved. At completion of the SU process, the request to initiate the project is forwarded to the Project Board (see figure 11.1).

How the SU process supports the PRINCE2 principles

The SU process supports all seven PRINCE2 principles:

- **Continued business justification** – In the Project Brief an outline Business Case is included.
- **Learn from experience** – Capture previous lessons is an explicit activity to be carried out in this process.
- **Defined roles and responsibilities** – The PMT structure and role descriptions are defined.
- **Manage by stages** – A detailed Stage Plan is defined for the next (initiation) stage.
- **Focus on products** – The Project Product Description is created in this process.
- **Manage by exception** – The project tolerances are captured in the Project Product Description.
- **Tailor to suit the project environment** – Approach, roles and responsibilities are suited to the project environment.

The activities within the SU process

The Starting up a Project process consists of the following activities:

Appoint Executive and Project Manager

First of all the Executive is appointed by the corporate or programme management based on the project mandate, and the Executive role description is created and confirmed. The Executive then establishes the role description for the Project Manager before selecting and appointing the Project Manager. The appointment of the Project Manager has to be confirmed by the respective corporate or programme management. For both roles the required investment in time for the project has to be defined. Finally the Project Manager creates the Daily Log as a repository for the project information that is not (yet) captured elsewhere.

Capture previous lessons

It can be important to learn from previous experience to help ensure that the project will be a success. If the strengths and weakness are known, as well as what works well and what doesn't, then better choices can be made.

Lessons can be captured not only from other projects or programmes, but also from the broader context of the company or from external organizations. The Project Manager creates the Lessons Log for the project.

Design and appoint project management team

The people in the project management team need to have sufficient knowledge and authority to be able to make the right decisions within the project. The composition of the project management team and, in particular, the composition of the Project Board, is therefore extremely important. Further, it is essential that all members of the project management team know what their role and accompanying responsibilities are, together with authorities and the associated communication and reporting lines.

The Project Manager creates the project management team structure and role descriptions, which have to be approved by the Executive. The Executive appoints the members of the project management team, and these have to be confirmed by the corporate or programme management.

Prepare outline Business Case

Besides the questions **what** and **how** things have to be done, it is important to concentrate too on **why** things are necessary. In the outline Business Case the focus is firmly on the reasons why the project is necessary, how the project contributes to the corporate or programme objectives and what kind of business options have been considered before choosing the selected alternative. Further considerations include how the project will be funded and what the major business risks are in relation to the project.

The Executive is responsible for the creation of the outline Business Case in consultation with the other Project Board members and the Project Manager. The outline Business Case has to be confirmed by the respective corporate or programme management. In parallel the Project Manager creates the Project Product Description in consultation with the Project Assurance. Sometimes the Executive delegates the actual preparation of the outline Business Case to the Project Manager.

Select project approach and assemble Project Brief

Before planning can commence in the initiation stage, there is a need to establish how the project output is to be achieved. Will the output be purchased, or will the work be carried out in-house or outsourced? Will existing products be used or will entirely new products be developed? And so on. All of this is captured in the project approach.

The Project Brief provides the project definition and the framework within which the project has to be implemented. The customer quality expectations and acceptance criteria (functional specifications) should be recorded and prioritized at this stage, as should the most significant risks. All these aspects form part of the Project Brief. The project approach is also part of the Project Brief.

The Project Manager selects the project approach and assembles the Project Brief. Additional role descriptions will be created if required.

Plan initiation stage

During the initiation stage, the Project Initiation Documentation is prepared and the Stage Plan for the first delivery stage is developed. It is important that it is established in advance exactly what needs to be delivered for this purpose and to what level of detail, who has to do what work, how reporting on this will be carried out, what needs to be ready by when and who has to review what for approval. All this needs to be captured in the Initiation Stage Plan.

The Project Manager is responsible for preparing the Initiation Stage Plan. After completion of the Project Brief and the Initiation Stage Plan, both are submitted to the Project Board for approval together with the request to initiate the project.

The purpose of a Project Brief (SU04)

The purpose of the Project Brief is to provide a full and firm basis for the initiation of the project. The Project Brief has to be discussed with all stakeholders to generate support and to manage expectations. The Project Brief has to be endorsed by all members of the Project Board to convince them that it is worthwhile commencing the project.

The responsibilities within the activities of the SU process

For an overview of the roles and responsibilities for the SU process, see table 11.1.

Table 11.1 Roles and responsibilities of the Starting up a Project process

Corporate / programme management	Project Manager (PM)
Corporate / programme management • Provide mandate • Create Executive role description • Appoint the Executive • Confirm appointment of selected members of PMT • Confirm (outline) Business Case **Executive** • Produce PM role description • Appoint the PM • Approve the PMT structure and role descriptions • Appoint selected members of PMT • Produce the (outline) Business Case • Review the Lessons Log **Senior User** • Review the (outline) Business Case from a user perspective **Senior Supplier** • Review the (outline) Business Case from a supplier perspective	**Project Manager (PM)** • Create and update Daily and Lessons Logs • Produce the PMT structure and role descriptions • Review the (outline) Business Case • Produce the Project Product Description • Produce the project approach • Assemble the Project Brief • Produce the initial Stage Plan • Forward request to initiate a project **Project Assurance** • Review the (outline) Business Case • Review the Project Product Description • Review the project approach and Project Brief • Review the initial Stage Plan

Multiple choice - Starting up a Project process

SU01. Which of the following best describes the purpose of the process Starting up a Project?
a. Sufficient information must be available to be able to define and confirm the scope of the project
b. Deciding on the project start is a matter for the Executive and Project Manager
c. The Business Case has to be clear in detail
d. Starting the project without hesitation

SU02. What question is most typically used for the process Starting up a Project?
a. Is the project well described?
b. Do we have a viable project?
c. Can we start the project without further delay?
d. Do we know what the project is about?

SU03. Which of the following is NOT an objective of the Starting up a Project process?
a. That the right authorities exist to start the project
b. That there is a business justification to initiate the project
c. To form the basis for the management and assessment of the project's overall success
d. That time is not wasted on projects that should not start at all

SU04. Which of the following is NOT a correct statement in relation to the Starting up a Project process?
a. This is the first process of the PRINCE2 process model
b. A mandate from the Executive is the trigger to start this process
c. This process triggers the process Directing a Project
d. The Project Brief and the Initiation Plan are deliverables of this process

SU05. How is the business justification principle supported by the Starting up a Project process?
a. Through preparing the Project Brief
b. Through appointing the Executive and Project Manager
c. Through creating the outline Business Case
d. Through capturing previous lessons

SU06. Which task is performed in the activity plan initiation stage?
a. To determine and agree the level of detail of the Project Plan
b. To prepare the outline Project Plan
c. To define the project approach
d. To prepare the first delivery stage

SU07. What best describes the purpose of the Project Brief?
a. To prepare a full and firm basis for discussion with the stakeholders about the project outlines
b. To prepare a full and firm basis for the delivery of the project
c. To prepare a full and firm basis between the Project Manager and the Executive about the project to be undertaken
d. To prepare a full and firm basis for the initiation of the project

12 Directing a Project (DP)

Purpose (DP01)

The purpose of the DP process is to make it possible for the Project Board to assume responsibility for the success of the project by taking the important decisions themselves, and to control the entire project.

Learning outcomes

Syllabus area	Topic	Topic description	Level
Understand the DP process and how it can be applied and tailored on a project. Specifically to identify:			
DP	01	The purpose of the DP process	2
DP	02	The objectives of the DP process	2
DP	03	The context of the DP process	2

Definitions

- **Acceptance** – The formal confirmation that the project product complies with the acceptance criteria and meets the requirements of the stakeholders.
- **Approval** – Formal confirmation that a project product is complete and complies with the criteria specified in the Product Description.
- **Authorization** – Formal confirmation that an authority is granted.
- **Exception assessment** – A review by the Project Board to authorize the Exception Plan.
- **End stage assessment** – A review by the Project Board to authorize the next Stage Plan.
- **Closure notification** – Advice from the Project Board to all stakeholders that the project is being closed and that the team members and supporting facilities are no longer required from a specific date.

The objectives of the DP process (DP02)

The objectives of the DP process are to ensure:
- There is an authority to initiate and to deliver the project products;
- Management direction and control are provided throughout the project and the project remains viable;
- There is an interface between corporate or programme management and the project;
- Plans for reviewing the benefits are produced and updated during the project;
- There is an authority to close the project.

The context of the DP process (DP03)

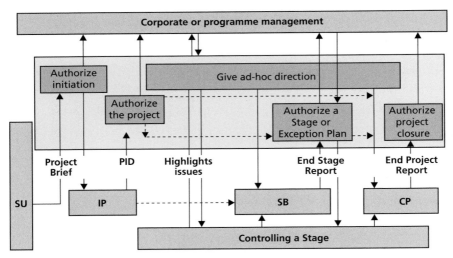

Figure 12.1 Overview of Directing a Project process (based on OGC PRINCE2 material)

The DP process starts on completion of the SU process and is triggered by the request to initiate the project by the Project Manager. The DP process does not cover the day-to-day management of the project, but encompass the directing of the project by the Project Board, with the focus on managing 'by exception'. The Project Board directs the project by means of a relatively small number of decision points. Regular progress meetings are unnecessary. The Project Manager informs the Project Board in between by Highlight Reports and only escalates exceptions to the agreed plan for decision(see figure 12.1).

The communication to and from the corporate or programme management and other stakeholders outside the project is an important task of the Project Board, and is specified in the Communication Management Strategy. A key role of the Project Board is to keep the respective corporate or programme management engaged with the project.

The Project Board should provide unified directions to the Project Manager via informal advice and guidance as well via formal directions. The Project Board is responsible for ensuring the continued business justification of the project.

How the DP process supports the PRINCE2 principles

The DP process supports all seven PRINCE2 principles:
- **Continued business justification** - The viability of the project is the leading principle in all of the Project Board's decisions.
- **Learn from experience** – By ensuring that lessons learned are incorporated as repeated issues in Project Board's assessments.

- **Defined roles and responsibilities** – By approving the PMT structure and role descriptions as defined.
- **Manage by stages** – By approving the individual Stage Plans separately from the (updated) Project Plan.
- **Focus on products** – By approving the (Project) Product Descriptions as part of the approval documents.
- **Manage by exception** – By defining the stage tolerances and ensuring stage tolerances are not exceeded.
- **Tailor to suit the project environment** – By ensuring that the project is tailored to the project environment.

The activities within the DP process

The Directing a Project process consists of the following activities:

Authorize initiation
Before execution of the initiation stage the Project Board must determine what the project entails, what work has to be carried out to execute the initiation and if such an investment is worthwhile at this moment.

Authorize project initiation is the first activity of the Directing a Project process and is triggered by the request of the Project Manager to initiate the project. Inputs for the activity authorize project initiation are the Project Brief and Initiation Stage Plan, developed in the SU process.

To authorize project initiation the Project Board must:
- Formally confirm the appointment of the project management team members and approve the role descriptions.
- Review, approve and have the Project Brief confirmed by the corporate or programme management, including the project approach, Project Product Description and outline Business Case.
- Review and approve the Initiation Stage Plan.
- Ensure the required resources for the execution of the Initiation Stage Plan will be available.
- Check whether the lessons learned from earlier projects are appropriately considered in the developed proposals.
- Authorize the Project Manager to start with the initiation stage of the project.
- Inform the host sites and other stakeholders of the authorization to start the initiation of the project via the initiation notification.

The above actions deliver the formal approval of the various documents, the authorization of the project start to the Project Manager and the announcement of the project start to the facilitating organization and other stakeholders.

Authorize the project
The costs of delivering a project can be considerable. Before the actual execution of the project can be started, it should be ensured that:

- There is an accepted Business Case for the project which indicates that the project is desirable, viable and feasible.
- The Project Plan is suitable for realizing the Business Case.
- The prepared strategies and controls support the execution of the Project Plan.
- The mechanisms to measure and review the envisaged benefits have been set up and planned.

The authorize the project activity is triggered by the request of the Project Manager to deliver the project. At authorization of the project, the Project Initiation Documentation and the Benefits Review Plan are approved and the execution of the project authorized. It must be checked whether the lessons learned and the strategies have been considered in the developed plans and if everyone knows and accepts their role. The corporate or programme management and other stakeholders are informed about the fact that the execution of the project and the first execution stage have been authorized.

At the same time as the authorize the project activity, the assessment of the Stage Plan for the first delivery stage and the assessment of the End Stage Report of the initiation stage are undertaken. The Project Board may decide to delegate a part of the assessment tasks to Project Assurance and approval authority on request for changes to a Change Authority.

Authorize a Stage or Exception Plan

It is important that the activities in a stage only start when the Project Board has explicitly authorized it. The Project Board has to re-assess at the end of every intermediate management stage the desirability, viability and feasibility of the project, and has to review the Stage Plan of the next stage before the execution of that stage is undertaken.

The activity, authorize a Stage or Exception Plan, is triggered by the request of the Project Manager to authorize the next Stage Plan or an Exception Plan. The Project Board uses the Stage Plan for the next stage or the Exception Plan, the End Stage Report for the current stage, the (updated) Benefits Review Plan and the (updated) Project Initiation Documentation as input for this activity.

The End Stage Report, inclusive of the updated Project Plan, Business Case and most important risks, is reviewed and approved. The Stage Plan for the next stage, inclusive of the Product Descriptions, is assessed and approved. The required resources for the execution of the next stage are ensured. Changes in the project management team are authorized. The possible update of the Project Initiation Documentation and Benefits Review Plan are reviewed and confirmed. The status of the project is communicated to the corporate or programme management and other stakeholders. A possible Lessons Report to the corporate or programme organization is assessed and approved.

This activity is also carried out when the project or stage tolerances look as though they may be exceeded and the Project Manager has produced an Exception Plan at the request of the Project Board. If project tolerances are likely to be exceeded, then the Project Board has to consult with the corporate or programme management in order to take a decision.

Give ad hoc direction

Even when the execution of a project stays within agreed tolerances, the Project Board has to react to escalated issues and risks. Decisions have to be taken on exceptions.

The Project Board receives regular Highlight Reports. In addition, the Project Board can receive informal requests for advice or guidance and formal Issue and Exceptions Reports from the Project Manager, and advice or directions from corporate or programme management.

The Project Board reviews the progress of the project by means of Highlight Reports, gaining assurance that the project is running according to plan and remains focused on the Business Case. If the Project Board feels there is an exceptional situation, they can ask the Project Manager to produce an Exception Report. The Project Board informs the corporate or programme management and other stakeholders on the progress of the project, as directed in the Communication Management Strategy.

In response to informal requests for advice and guidance, the Project Board should assist the Project Manager accordingly. The Project Board can seek advice from the corporate or programme management if necessary.

In response to an escalated Issue Report, the Project Board has to take a direct decision. The Board can also request more information, ask corporate or programme management for advice or a decision, or can defer the decision to a later moment in time. If the Project Board expects that stage or project tolerances are exceeded, the Board can ask the Project Manager to forward an Exception Report.

In response to an Exception Report, the Project Board can take a qualified decision and ask the Project Manager to develop this decision into an Exception Plan or instruct the Project Manager to close the project prematurely. The Board can also defer the decision to a later moment in time. In case there is a risk that the project tolerances might be exceeded, the Project Board has to escalate the Exception Report to corporate or programme management for a decision.

In response to advice and decisions from corporate or programme management, the Board has to inform the project management team accordingly, notify the Project Manager on any changes that may affect the project, and ensure that appropriate actions are taken.

Authorize project closure

The decision to close a project is just as important as the decision to start it. It must be determined that continuation of the project no longer provides any added value for the organization within the agreed Business Case. Otherwise, a project will continue forever.

With closure, it should be checked whether the objectives of the project have been realized and the extent to which the result deviates from what was originally agreed. The initial and final version of the Project Initiation Documentation should be reviewed to understand (the difference between) the original baseline and the current situation.

The Project Board must further ensure that:
- An operational and maintenance organization is in place for the products to be delivered.
- The user acceptance and operational and maintenance acceptance are formally confirmed, thereby ensuring that all acceptance criteria of the project products to be handed over have been satisfied.
- All products to be delivered have been formally handed over to operation and maintenance in accordance with the Configuration Management Strategy.
- The End Project Report is reviewed and approved, including the Lessons Learned Report and the follow-on action recommendations. The Project Board should also identify the authorities within the corporate or programme management who should take the identified recommendations forward.
- The Benefits Review Plan is updated for post-project benefits reviews and transferred to corporate or programme management.
- The Business Case is updated to serve as the basis for the post-project benefits reviews.
- A project closure notification is issued to all parties concerned, in accordance with the Communication Management Strategy, with advice to all suppliers that they can withdraw all infrastructure and resources provided. The notification should also include a closing date for costs being charged to the project.
- The Project Manager is discharged.

The authorize project closure activity is initiated by the Project Manager as part of the Closing a Project process. It comprises the closing activities of the Project Board in relation to the project. The Project Board can decide to delegate a part of the associated assessment tasks to Project Assurance.

The responsibilities within the activities of the DP process

For an overview of the roles and responsibilities for the DP process, see table 12.1.

Table 12.1 Roles and responsibilities of the Directing a Project process

Corporate / programme management	Project Assurance
<ul><li>Confirm the Project Brief</li><li>Confirm the (updated) PID</li><li>Confirm (updated) Business Case</li><li>Confirm (updated) Benefits Review Plan</li><li>Advise / raise new issues</li><li>Direct on project level exceptions</li></ul>**Executive/ Project Board**<ul><li>Approve the Project Brief and initial Stage Plan</li><li>Review Lessons Log</li><li>Approve (updated) PID</li><li>Review (Project Board) and approve (Executive) Business Case and Benefits Review Plan</li><li>Give ad hoc advice and guidance</li><li>Review Highlight Reports</li><li>Confirm approval of specialist products</li><li>Review and respond on Exception Reports</li><li>Approve End Stage Reports, Stage/ Exception Plans</li><li>Approve End Project Report</li><li>Approve Lessons Report and follow-on action recommendations</li></ul>	<ul><li>Review the Project Brief and initial Stage Plan</li><li>Review Lessons Log</li><li>Review (updated) PID and Benefits Review Plan</li><li>Review Highlight / Exception Reports</li><li>Review End Stage Reports, Stage / Exception Plans</li><li>Review End Project Report and (updated) Business Case</li><li>Review Lessons Report and follow-on action recommendations</li></ul>**Project Manager (PM)**<ul><li>Deliver all input to the Project Board</li><li>Request for advice and decisions</li><li>Triggers for authorizations</li></ul>

Multiple choice - Directing a Project process

DP01. What best describes the purpose of the Directing a Project process?
a. To direct and control the entire project
b. Taking responsibility for the success of the project
c. To ensure that the project will be delivered in line with the objectives set
d. Manage the project by exception

DP02. What phrase best describes the Directing a Project process?
a. Management by taking accountability
b. Management and control
c. Management of success
d. Management by exception

DP03. Which of the following is NOT an objective of the Directing a Project process?
a. Direction and control are provided throughout the project
b. Providing an interface with corporate or programme management
c. Delegating the day-to-day management to the Project Manager
d. Plans for reviewing the benefits are produced and updated during the project

DP04. What document is NOT an input for authorizing project initiation?
a. Project Initiation Documentation
b. Project Brief
c. Initiation Stage Plan
d. Lessons Log

DP05. The activity give ad hoc direction is an example of what principle?
a. Continuous business justification
b. Commitment and involvement
c. Management by exception
d. Management by walking around

DP06. Who is responsible for ratifying the PID?
a. Project Manager
b. Project Board
c. Corporate or programme management
d. Project Assurance

DP07. Fill in the blank in the following sentence with the right product.
The [?] is reviewed by the Project Board and approved by the Executive.
a. Business Case
b. Follow-on recommendations
c. End Stage Report
d. Exception Plan

13 Initiating a Project (IP)

Purpose (IP01)

The purpose of the Initiating a Project process is to lay a good foundation for the project, which enables the organization to become aware of the work that has to be done in order to deliver the project result, before considerable expenditure is committed.

Learning outcomes

Syllabus area	Topic	Topic description	Level
Understand the IP process and how it can be applied and tailored on a project. Specifically to identify:			
IP	01	The purpose of the IP process	2
IP	02	The objectives of the IP process	2
IP	03	The context of the IP process	2
IP	04	The purpose of the Project Initiation Documentation (PID)	2

Definitions

- **Corporate or programme standard** – An over-arching standard from the corporate or programme organization to which the project strategies and controls must comply.
- **Strategy** – An approach or direction to take in order to achieve long-term goals.
- **PID** – The collection of documents that contain the key information needed to start the project on a sound basis and that convey the information to all concerned with the project.
- **Benefits Review Plan** – A plan that indicates how, when and by whom the benefits that are to be realized will be measured.

The objectives of the IP process (IP02)

The objectives of the IP process are to ensure that there is a common understanding of:
- Why the project is needed, the benefits expected and the associated risks;
- The scope and the products to be delivered;
- How, when and what is to be delivered, and at what costs;
- How the required quality is to be achieved and assured;
- How baselines will be established and controlled, and how changes and issues will be managed;
- How progress will be monitored, reported and controlled;
- Who needs what information, when and in which format;
- How the corporate or programme standards will be tailored to this project.

The context of the IP process (IP03)

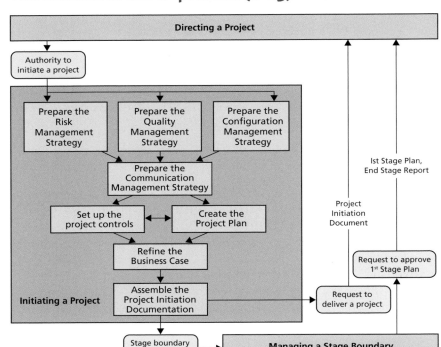

Figure 13.1 Overview of theInitiating a Project process (based on OGC PRINCE2 material)

For a successful project, it must be clear to all parties before any work is started exactly what the project is expected to achieve, why it is necessary, how the results are to be realized and what the responsibilities of all the parties involved are. In this way commitment is created. The IP process provides such a basis for a project.

The IP process commences as soon as the Project Board authorizes initiation by approving the Project Brief and the Initiation Stage Plan.

The IP process is the first process in the project. The first process in the PRINCE2 process model is Starting up a Project, but this process takes place before the actual start of the project.

The IP process is triggered by the authorization of the Project Board. The IP process starts with the creation of the Risk, Quality, Configuration and Communication Management Strategies, and the respective logs and registers. The Project Plan is produced and the project controls are agreed. The Business Case is refined and the Benefits Review Plan is prepared. Finally the Project Initiation Documentation is assembled and the request to deliver a project is forwarded to the Project Board. The assembling of the PID also triggers the Managing a Stage Boundary process to prepare the Stage Plan for the first delivery stage, and to prepare the End Stage Report so that the Initiation Stage can be reviewed (see figure 13.1).

The IP process ensures that the project is viable and in line with business and programme objectives. The IP process also ensures that the members of the Project Board become the owners of the project.

How the IP process supports the PRINCE2 principles

The IP process supports all seven PRINCE2 principles:
- **Continued business justification** – The outline Business Case is refined.
- **Learn from experience** – All strategies and controls are prepared based on corporate or programme management standards and Lesson Reports from previous projects.
- **Defined roles and responsibilities** – The (updated) PMT structure and role descriptions are captured in the PID, whilst the Communication Management Strategy is also defined.
- **Manage by stages** – The management stages are defined and recorded in the Project Plan.
- **Focus on products** – The Project Product Description is updated and recorded in the Project Plan. The Stage Plan for the first delivery stage records the respective Project Descriptions of the products to be delivered.
- **Manage by exception** – The controls and the project and stage tolerances are defined to suit the manage by exception principle. Effective controls are fundamental for this principle.
- **Tailor to suit the project environment** – The agreed tailoring of this project is recorded in the PID.

The activities within the IP process

The Initiating a Project process consists of the following activities:

Preparing the Risk Management Strategy
The Risk Management Strategy describes the objectives, procedures, responsibilities and techniques for the application of risk management. It is, therefore, all about the way in which risk management is applied within the project, providing the framework for risk tolerance and the instances when risks must be analyzed and reported.

The Risk Management Strategy is formulated by the Project Manager and approved by the Project Board. The Executive is ultimately responsible for risk management within the project. Parallel to the Risk Management Strategy, the Risk Register is created. Risks that are already recorded in the Daily Log are recorded into the newly created Risk Register. Preparing the strategy and creating the Risk Register is reviewed by Project Assurance.

Prepare the Configuration Management Strategy
The Configuration Management Strategy provides the project with the ability to control its baselined products effectively. Exactly what must be controlled under configuration management, and at what level of detail, differs in every project. In the Configuration Management Strategy the objectives, procedures and techniques for the application of configuration management are specified. In this strategy the change and issue procedures are also defined.

The Configuration Management Strategy is produced by the Project Manager and approved by the Project Board. Parallel to this, the Issue Register and the database for the Configuration Item Records are created. Issues already recorded in the Daily Log, which should be managed formally, are also recorded in the Issue Register. Preparing the strategy and creating the Issue Register and the Configuration Item Records are reviewed by Project Assurance.

Prepare the Quality Management Strategy
The delivery of the project output according to customer quality expectations and acceptance criteria is a critical success criterion for a project. There needs to be agreement between the customer and supplier on how to manage quality. Like other strategies the objectives, procedures, responsibilities and techniques for the application of quality management are recorded in the Quality Management Strategy. The Quality Management Strategy will state whether to use the quality system of the customer, the supplier's, or a combination of these.

The Quality Management Strategy is prepared by the Project Manager and approved by the Project Board. In parallel to the Quality Management Strategy, the Quality Register is created.

Prepare the Communication Management Strategy
Communication is crucial for the alignment between the project and its environment. The Communication Management Strategy defines what the key concepts in communication are, how often communications should take place, by whom, to whom and how the communication should be undertaken.

The Communication Management Strategy is co-determined by the Risk Management, Configuration Management and Quality Management Strategies. The Communication Management Strategy is defined by the Project Manager and approved by the Project Board.

Set up project controls
Every decision in the project must be considered carefully and taken in a timely manner. This can only be done if the decision-makers have the correct information at their disposal. Control mechanisms help to ensure that every level of the project management team can:
• Assess the progress;
• Compare the progress with the plan;
• Test plans and options on the basis of different scenarios;
• Map out problems;
• Take corrective actions and authorize follow-on activities.

The project controls describe the way in which issues and escalations are dealt with, what the tolerances for the different levels are, and also how responsibilities and authorities are delegated. The project controls are prepared by the Project Manager and approved by the Project Board.

Create the Project Plan
The Project Plan is an outline plan covering the total delivery stage(s) of the project. The Project Plan defines the products to be delivered, when and at what cost, and the resources needed to carry out the work required. As part of the Project Plan, the Project Product Description is updated and the relevant Product Descriptions are defined.

The Project Plan provides input to the Business Case and is an essential component of the Project Initiation Documentation. The Project Plan is prepared by the Project Manager and is approved by the Project Board.

For this and the previous activities, it may be necessary to update the PMT structure and the respective role descriptions. In addition, the Issue and Risk Registers may need to be updated.

Refine the Business Case

In the IP process, the Business Case is refined. The validity of the basic assumptions on which the outline Business Case was based, must be tested. In addition the Benefits Review Plan should also be created. How, when and who measures, records and reviews the achievement of the individual benefits? What are the actual baselines?

The Business Case and the Benefits Review Plan are prepared under the responsibility of the Project Manager and approved by the Project Board. However, the work is often actually done by business analysts from corporate or programme management. It is also important to involve Project Assurance. The Executive has to have the baselines confirmed by the corporate or programme management.

Assemble the Project Initiation Documentation

There needs to be one comprehensive set of documents that contains all relevant information on the 'what, why, who, how, where, when and how much' of the project. This is the Project Initiation Documentation (PID). The PID can consist of a set of separate documents, can be one integrated document, or can be just a summary of the individual documents that have been prepared. At all times a management summary must be included to facilitate review and approval of the PID.

The PID is assembled by the Project Manager. After completion, the PID is submitted to the Project Board for approval together with the request to deliver the project. Often the Executive also has to have the PID confirmed by the corporate or programme management, but this is not a PRINCE2 requirement. The Project Assurance should be consulted in advance to ensure that the PID meets the needs of the individual members of the Project Board and the corporate or programme management.

During the assembling of the PID, the Managing a Stage Boundary process has to be triggered. In addition to the approval of the PID by the Project Board at the authorizing of the project, the Stage Plan for the first delivery stage also has to be approved and the performance of the work in the initiation stage has to be reviewed.

The purpose of the Project Initiation Documentation (IP04)

The purpose of the PID is to define the project, thereby creating a basis for the delivery of the project and the subsequent assessment of its overall success. The PID:
- Ensures there is a sound basis for the project before major commitments are made;
- Acts as a basis for assessing the progress and the ongoing viability of the project;
- Provides a single source of reference about the project.

The responsibilities within the activities of the IP process

For an overview of the roles and responsibilities for the IP process, see table 13.1.

Table 13.1 Roles and responsibilities of the Initiating a Project process

| Project Manager (PM)
• Create the Risk, Quality, Configuration and Communication Management Strategies
• Approve the Risk, Issue and Quality Registers
• Approve the Configuration Item Records
• Update the PMT structure and role descriptions
• Create the Project Plan and Product Descriptions and update the Project Product Description
• Set up the project controls
• Refine the Business Case and create the Benefits Review Plan
• Assemble the Project Initation Documentation

Project Support
• Create, populate and update the Risk Register
• Create, populate and update the Issue Register
• Create and update the Configuration Item Records
• Create the Quality Register | Project Assurance
• Review the Risk, Quality, Configuration and Communication Management Strategies
• Review the Risk, Issue and Quality Register
• Review the Configuration Item Records
• Review the role descriptions
• Review the Project Plan and Product Descriptions and the updated Project Product Description
• Review the project controls
• Review the Business Case and Benefits Review Plan
• Review the Project Initation Documentation |

Multiple choice - Initiating a Project process

IP01. The stated purpose of the Initiating a Project process is:
a. Becoming aware of the work that has to be done to deliver the project result
b. Making it possible for the Project Board to take responsibility for the success of the project
c. Making sure that we have a viable project that is worth the effort
d. Providing the Project Board with sufficient information to approve the Stage Plan of the next stage, review the revised Project Plan, confirm the justification of the project and accept the risks

IP02. Which of the following best describes the Initiating a Project process?
a. Starting the delivery of the project
b. Accepting responsibility for the project
c. Laying the foundation for the project
d. Determining and describing the end goal of the project

IP03. Which of the following is NOT an objective of the Initiating a Project process?
a. To determine how progress will be monitored, reported and controlled
b. To determine who needs what information, when and in which format
c. To determine how benefits will be realized based on the project result to be delivered
d. To determine how the corporate or programme standards will be tailored to this project

IP04. Which of the following is NOT an objective of the Project Initiation Documentation?
a. To create a basis for the delivery of the project
b. To create a continuously updated actual status of the project
c. To create a single source of reference about the project
d. To create a basis for the assessment of the overall success of the project

IP05. How does the Initiating a Project process support the manage by stages principle?
a. By defining the management stages in the Project Plan
b. By controlling the present stage on a detailed basis
c. By developing the Stage Plan for the next stage alongside an update of the Project Plan
d. By approving the individual Stage Plans

IP06. Which management product contains all the relevant information about the project?
a. Project plan
b. Project Initiation Documentation
c. Project Product Description
d. Project controls

IP07. Which PRINCE2 role is responsible for setting up the project controls?
a. Project Board
b. Project Manager
c. Project Assurance
d. Project Support

IP08. Fill in the blank in the following sentence with the right product.

The [?] is created by Project Support, approved by the Project Manager, and reviewed by Project Assurance.

a. Risk Management Strategy
b. Role descriptions
c. Product Descriptions
d. Configuration Item Records

14 Controlling a Stage (CS)

Purpose (CS01)

The purpose of the Controlling a Stage (CS) process is the assignment and monitoring of the work to be completed, dealing with issues, reporting on progress to the Project Board and the execution of corrective actions so that the project remains within the agreed tolerances.

Learning outcomes

Syllabus area	Topic	Topic description	Level
Understand the CS process and how it can be applied and tailored on a project. Specifically to identify:			
CS	01	The purpose of the CS process	2
CS	02	The objectives of the CS process	2
CS	03	The context of the CS process	2

Definitions

- **Corrective action** – An action to resolve a threat to a plan's tolerance or an off-specification to a product.
- **Exception Report** – A report in which an exception is described, including the (impact of the) recommendation.
- **Highlight Report** – An outline report on the progress of a stage that the Project Manager provides to the Project Board and other stakeholders at predetermined times.

The objectives of the CS process (CS02)

The objectives of the CS process are to ensure that the stage products are delivered:
- To stated quality standards, on time and within budget;
- In a controlled manner, avoiding uncontrolled change (scope creep) and loss of focus;
- With risks and issues kept under control;
- In support of the defined benefits and with the Business Case remaining viable;
- Ultimately with all performance targets achieved within the agreed tolerances.

The context of the CS process (CS03)

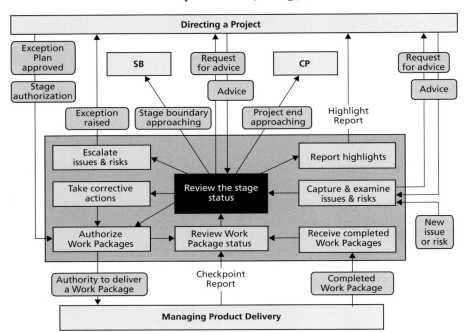

Figure 14.1 Overview of Controlling a Stage process (based on OGC PRINCE2 material)

The Controlling a Stage process starts when the Project Board authorizes the stage or approves the Exception Plan. These triggers initiate the initial 'authorize a Work Package' in the stage concerned.

In the Controlling a Stage process the Project Manager directs the Team Manager whose activities are described in the Managing Product Delivery process. The interfaces between the two processes are specified in the activities authorize a Work Package, review the Work Package status and receive completed Work Packages.

Capture and examine issues and risks is defined as a separate activity. The review the stage status activity initiates the corrective actions to be taken. During the activities capture and examine issues and risks and review the stage status, the Project Manager can request advice from the Project Board. The review of the stage status also initiates the processes Managing a Stage Boundary (SB) and Closure of a Project (CP).

The Project Manager reports periodically to the Project Board by means of Highlight Reports. If the Project Manager expects the agreed tolerances to be exceeded, this is reported in an Exception Report to the Project Board in the escalate issues and risks activity (see figure 14.1).

In the CS process all the principles are clearly integrated in the activities. It describes the day-to-day management activities of the Project Manager during the different stages of the project.

As soon as the execution of a stage has been authorized by the Project Board, and the required resources have been released, the project management team must concentrate on the delivery of the agreed product and services in accordance with the quality requirements stated, on time and within budget.

How the CS process supports the PRINCE2 principles

The CS process supports all seven PRINCE2 principles:
- **Continued business justification** - Is reviewed at review stage status and during the examining risks and issues activity.
- **Learn from experience** – Is an issue at every review of the stage status and in the Highlight Report.
- **Defined roles and responsibilities** – Any change in the PMT during the stage will be captured as an issue.
- **Manage by stages** – Controls the present stage on a detailed basis.
- **Focus on products** – All stage management baselines and reports are product based.
- **Manage by exception** – Regular Highlight Reports are prepared. Exception Reports are issued only when there is a risk that stage tolerances will be exceeded.
- **Tailor to suit the project environment** – Work Packages are tailored to suit the project environment.

The daily management of the project in the CS process is based fundamentally on the manage by stages principle.

The activities within the CS process

The Controlling a Stage process consists of the following activities:

Authorize Work Packages
Chaos is created in a project when everyone starts activities whenever they personally consider it appropriate. Therefore work should only start when the Project Manager has explicitly agreed this with the relevant Team Manager in a Work Package. The authorize Work Package activity is triggered by the stage authorization or approval of the Exception Plan by the Project Board and by corrective actions taken by the Project Manager.

The Project Manager should check the Stage Plan and the different strategies and controls in the Project Initiation Documentation in order to understand the arrangements needed for a specific Work Package, before that Work Package can be authorized.

A (description of the) Work Package contains amongst other things:
- The description of the work to be done;
- The product descriptions of the products to be delivered, including the quality requirements;
- The joint agreement on effort, cost, start and end dates, and key milestones of the work;
- Tolerances, constraints and the development, operations and maintenance interfaces;

- Configuration requirements, and change and escalation procedures;
- Reporting arrangements.

The Project Manager should review the Work Package with the Team Manager to ensure that it is acceptable and that work on the Work Package can be authorized to commence. The Project Manager should review the (extract of the) Team Plan with the Team Manager to ensure that the Team Plan links up with the Stage Plan. As more information is understood about the deliverables, or as risks and issues arise, the Project Manager must adapt the Stage Plan accordingly (within the tolerances), or escalate to the Project Board. The Project Manager should also update the status of the products in the Configuration Item Records, update the planned quality reviews in the Quality Register and update the Risk and Issue Registers as appropriate.

The Product Descriptions of the products to be delivered form the basis of the Work Package. The authorize a Work Package activity provides the formal transfer of the Work Package to the Team Manager.

Review Work Package status

In order to be able to manage a project, the Project Manager should know the status of the different Work Packages in relation to the Stage Plan. The Stage Plan should be updated, with the actuals, forecasts and adjustments incorporated. The Project Manager monitors the progress of the stage based on Checkpoint Reports and the progress reviews with the Team Managers. The Project Manager also makes use of the entries in the Quality Register and the Configuration Item Records. If necessary, the Issue and Risk Registers are updated.

Capture and examine issues and risks

Issues and risks can occur in the project at any time. Issues and risks can be generated by anyone with an interest in the project. All issues and risks should be recorded. Issues that can be dealt informally are recorded in the Daily Log. Issues that should be dealt formally are recorded in the Issue Register. All risks are recorded in the Risk Register. The impact should be analyzed for all issues and risks. For each entry in the Issue Register a separate Issue Report is prepared.

The Project Manager is responsible for capturing and examining all of the issues and risks. If necessary, the Project Manager can be supported by the Team Managers and Project Assurance and can ask for advice from the individual members of the Project Board. The administrative activities can be delegated to Project Support.

Review the stage status

If the status of the work during a project is not regularly reviewed, the project will not be under control and, hence, there is an increased chance of failure. In order to avoid this, it is important that a regular assessment of the status of the work is undertaken with reference to the approved plan. Based on this it can be decided whether the next Work Package can be started, whether any corrective action should be taken, whether issues and risks should be escalated and if the Managing a Stage Boundary or Closing a Project processes should be initiated.

Review the Work Package status and capture and examine issues and risks are inputs for the review of the stage status. During the review of the stage status the respective logs and registers are updated.

The Project Manager is responsible for reviewing the status of the stage. If necessary the Project Manager can be supported by Project Support and Project Assurance, and can ask for advice from the individual members of the Project Board.

Take corrective actions

The Project Manager captures the necessary information and selects the optimal option. The Project Manager updates the Stage Plan, including the relevant Product Descriptions and Configuration Item Records. The Project Manager informs the stakeholders concerned and then finally initiates the corrective action. The Project Manager updates the respective logs and registers.

Taking corrective actions is initiated from the activity review the stage status. The take corrective action activity initiates the authorize a Work Package activity.

Report highlights

An update from the Project Manager to the Project Board and other stakeholders will keep them informed and involved in the project, and enables the Project Board to exert its responsibilities. For this the Project Manager periodically informs the Project Board via a Highlight Report. The frequency of the Highlight Report is specified during the IP process and is established in the Project Initiation Documentation.

The Project Manager makes use of the actuals in the available reports, plans and registers, and the preceding Highlight Report. The Project Manager captures the information required, creates a Highlight Report for the current period and ensures distribution in accordance with what has been agreed in the Communication Management Strategy.

Escalate issues and risks

If one or more agreed tolerances are in danger of being exceeded, the Project Manager should escalate an Exception Report to the Project Board.

In the Exception Report, the Project Manager describes the cause of the exception, the possible consequences, the available options and their consequences, and any lessons learned, and advises the board on which option seems to be the most appropriate. The consequences on the Stage and Project Plans, the Business Case and the risks and tolerances are taken into account for the cause of the exception and for each option.

Receive completed Work Packages

If work is being delivered by external providers, it will always be necessary to formally test if this work has been completed, accepted and handed over correctly before discharge can be given to the supplier. The same actions are necessary to assure a successful delivery of the Work Package when it is handed over by the Team Manager.

The Project Manager should ensure that all quality assessments of the deliverable products have been executed, that all criteria have been satisfied and that all deliverable products have been accepted by the responsible persons. The Project Manager needs to ensure that the entries in the Quality Register have been completed, the Configuration Item Records are updated and all completed products have been handed over to the configuration management.

The responsibilities within the activities of the CS process

For an overview of the roles and responsibilities for the CS process, see table 14.1.

Table 14.1 Roles and responsibilities of the Controlling a Stage process

Project Manager (PM)	Project Assurance
• Create Work Packages	• Review the new Work Packages
• Update status of Stage Plan	• Review updated Stage Plan
• Update Daily and Lessons Logs	• Review updated Issue and Risk Registers
• Review Team Plan and Checkpoint Reports	• Review Issue Reports
• Update Issue and Risk Registers	• Review updated Quality Register
• Produce Issue Reports if needed	• Review updated Configuration Item Records
• Review updated Quality Register	• Review Highlight Reports
• Approve (updated) Configuration Item Records	• Review Exception Reports
• Create Highlight Reports	
• Create Exception Reports	**Project Support**
• Review Product Status Account	• Update Configuration Item Records
	• Update Quality Register
	• Produce Product Status Account

Multiple choice - Controlling a Stage process

CS01. The purpose of the Controlling a Stage process is NOT:
a. The assignment and monitoring of the work to be completed
b. Reporting on progress to the Project Board
c. Escalating issues for advice and direction
d. Drafting Exception Plans to stay on track

CS02. Which of the following best describes the Controlling a Stage process?
a. Authorizing delivery stages
b. Delivering the products according to the Stage Plan
c. Reviewing the status of the project
d. Authorizing Work Packages

CS03. Which of the following is NOT an objective of the Controlling a Stage process?
a. To avoid uncontrolled change (scope creep)
b. To keep risks and issues under control
c. To ensure the defined benefits remain valid
d. To remain within the agreed tolerances

CS04. The Controlling a Stage process can be triggered by?
a. Authorize the project
b. The end of Initiating a Project
c. The end of Managing Stage Boundaries
d. Exception Plan approved

CS05. The daily management of the project in the Controlling a Stage process is based on the fundamental principle of?
a. Management by stages
b. Continuous business justification
c. A clear start and end
d. Management by exception

CS06. For assessing progress, the Project Manager compares the Stage Plan with the output of what?
a. Highlight Report
b. Escalate issues and risks
c. Review Work Package status
d. Receive completed Work Packages

CS07. What is a responsibility of the Project Manager in authorizing Work Packages?
a. Appointing the Team Manager
b. Setting the stage tolerances correctly for the Team Manager
c. Making sure the Team Manager accepts the Work Package
d. Ensuring the Work Package is part of the Team Plan

CS08. The Checkpoint Reports are an important input for which document?
a. End Stage Report
b. Issue Report
c. Quality Report
d. Highlight Report

CS09. Updating the Issue and Risk Registers are the responsibility of who?
a. Project Manager
b. Project Support
c. Project Assurance
d. Team Manager

15 Managing Product Delivery (MP)

Purpose (MP01)

The purpose of the Managing Product Delivery (MP) process is to control the relationship between the Project Manager and the Team Manager(s) by setting formal requirements for acceptance, execution and delivery of the project work.

Learning outcomes

Syllabus area	Topic	Topic description	Level
Understand the MP process and how it can be applied and tailored on a project. Specifically to identify:			
MP	01	The purpose of the MP process	2
MP	02	The objectives of the MP process	2
MP	03	The context of the MP process	2

Definitions

- **Team Plan** – An optional level of plan for the delivery of a Work Package.
- **Checkpoint Report** – A report on the progress of a Work Package that the Team Manager provides to the Project Manager at predetermined times.

The objectives of the MP process (MP02)

The objectives of the MP process are to ensure that:
- The work to be executed is agreed and authorized;
- It is clear to Team Managers what must be delivered, when, at what costs and with what resources;
- The planned products are delivered in accordance with the agreed specifications and within the agreed tolerances;
- Accurate progress information is provided to the Project Manager at agreed times to ensure that the expectations are met.

The context of the MP process (MP03)

The purpose of the Managing Product Delivery process is to control the way in which the Project Manager assigns activities to the Team Manager based on detailed Work Packages and the way in which these Work Packages are accepted, executed and delivered. The Managing Product Delivery process has a direct link with the Controlling a Stage process. The CS process is the responsibility of the Project Manager, while activities of the MP process are the responsibility of the Team Manager.

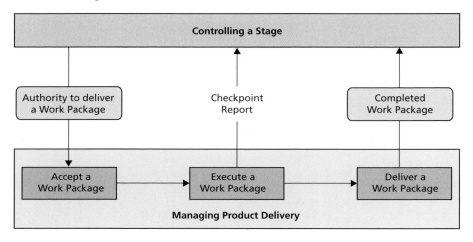

Figure 15.1 Overview of the Managing Product Delivery process (based on OGC PRINCE2 material)

The Managing Product Delivery process starts with the acceptance of the Work Package by the Team Manager from the Project Manager. The Team Manager executes the works defined in the Work Package, makes sure that the delivered products are reviewed and reports progress to the Project Manager. Finally the Team Manager notifies the Project Manager that all products have been handed over to configuration management and the Work Package has been completed (see figure 15.1).

In terms of the process, it does not matter if the Team Manager is from an external supplier or from an internal department of the customer. The work relationship between the Project Manager and the Team Manager can best be described as a relationship between the Project Manager and a preferred supplier. The activities described in this process can ideally be used to define the interface with an external company that makes no use of the PRINCE2 method.

How the MP process supports the PRINCE2 principles

The MP process supports all seven PRINCE2 principles:
- **Continued business justification** – Is an attention point in the tolerances set in the Work Package.
- **Learn from experience** – Possible lessons are reported in the Checkpoint Reports.
- **Defined roles and responsibilities** – Is defined in the authorized Work Packages.
- **Manage by stages** – Managing product delivery by Work Packages facilitates stage planning and delivery.

- **Focus on products** – Work Package, Team Plan and Checkpoint Reports are product based.
- **Manage by exception** – Work Package tolerances are escalation procedures and are captured in the Work Package.
- **Tailor to suit the project environment** – Work Packages are tailored to suit the project environment.

The Managing Product Delivery process is based fundamentally on the focus on products principle.

The activities within the MP process

The Managing Product Delivery process consists of the following activities.

Accept a Work Package

Before execution of the activities can be started, there must firstly be an agreement between the Project Manager and the Team Manager about the work to be carried out and the products to be delivered. The Team Manager has an individual responsibility in respect of the technical and commercial feasibility of the work to be undertaken. The Team Manager is accountable to the Senior Supplier, who has made the (contract) agreements with the customer for the realization of the delivered products.

To be able to accept accountability for the Work Package, the Team Manager should usually produce a Team Plan. This Team Plan may have been prepared already in the respective Stage Plan or it could be part of the Accept a Work Package activity. The Team Manager discusses the Team Plan and the associated risks with the Project Manager. With the acceptance of the Work Package, the Team Manager can then update the Team Plan if required. The Team Manager oversees the update of the Quality Register with data from the (updated) Team Plan.

Execute a Work Package

The Team Manager has to realize the products to be delivered in accordance with the Work Package and has to manage the interfaces that need to be taken into account. The Team Manager has to ensure that the activities are carried out within the agreed tolerances of time, money and quality, and has to escalate issues, risks and lessons learned to the Project Manager.

Execute a Work Package also includes the testing, obtaining of approval and acceptance of the products to be delivered. The approval records should be obtained and the update of the Quality Register and Configuration Item Records should be monitored. The Team Manager reports via the Checkpoint Reports to the Project Manager at the frequency agreed in the Work Package. The Team Manager should liaise with the Project Assurance about the realization of the specialist products, the progress achieved and the approval records to be obtained.

Deliver a Work Package

The Team Manager checks if all related actions from the Quality Register have been executed and if all products to be delivered have been approved and accepted. He/she also checks whether all quality files have been handed over to Project Support and if the Quality Register and the Configuration Item Records have been updated accordingly.

The Team Manager hands over the completed products to configuration management and notifies the Project Manager accordingly to obtain discharge for the Work Package concerned. The Team Manager updates the Team Plan to indicate that the Work Package has been completed. The Team Manager should liaise with Project Assurance to ensure that all actions which have been carried out conform with the procedures detailed in the Work Package.

The responsibilities within the activities of the MP process

For an overview of the roles and responsibilities for the MP process, see table 15.1.

Table 15.1 Roles and responsibilities for the Managing Product Delivery process

Team Manager (TM)	Project Assurance
• Produce and update the Team Plan	• Review (updated) Team Plan
• Accept, execute and deliver Work Package	• Review (updated) Work Package
• Raise issues and risks	• Review Checkpoint Reports
• Produce Checkpoint Reports	• Review specialist products
• Realize the specialist products	• Review approval records
• Obtain approval records	• Review and update Quality Register
• Review and update Quality Register	• Review Configuration Item Records
• Review and update Configuration Item Records	
• Deliver Work Package	**Project Support (as part of CS process)**
	• Review the approval records
	• Update the Quality Register
	• Update Configuration Item Records

Multiple choice - Managing Product Delivery process

MP01. The stated purpose of the Managing Product Delivery process is?
a. To control the relationship between the Project Manager and the Team Manager(s)
b. The delivery of (a part of) the stage products to the stated quality standards, on time and within budget
c. The assignment and monitoring of the work to be completed
d. To execute the works defined in the Work Package

MP02. Which of the following is NOT an objective of the Managing Product Delivery process?
a. The work to be executed is agreed and authorized
b. The planned products are delivered in accordance with the agreed specifications and within the agreed tolerances
c. Deviations from the planned schedule will be handled by the Team Manager on his own
d. Accurate progress information is provided to the Project Manager at agreed times to ensure that the expectations are met

MP03. The work relationship between the Project Manager and the Team Manager is ideally intended for:
a. Outsourcing work to preferred suppliers
b. Defining work for internal parties
c. External parties, who make use of the PRINCE2 method
d. All cases of project work that have to be delegated by the Project Manager

MP04. What principle best describes the Managing Product Delivery process?
a. Focus on product delivery
b. Continuous business justification
c. Management by stages
d. Management by exception

MP05. When the tolerances in the Team Plan appear to have been exceeded, what is the first thing the Team Manager has to do?
a. Report it in the Checkpoint Report
b. Escalate an issue
c. Inform the Project Assurance
d. Adjust the Team Plan

MP06. Who is responsible for updating the Quality Register during executing a Work Package?
a. Project Manager
b. Team Manager
c. Project Support
d. Quality assurance

16 Managing a Stage Boundary (SB)

Purpose (SB01)

The purpose of the Managing a Stage Boundary (SB) process is to provide the Project Board with sufficient information from the Project Manager so they can review the success of the current stage, approve the Stage Plan for the next stage, review the revised Project Plan, confirm the justification of the project and accept the risks.

Learning outcomes

Syllabus area	Topic	Topic description	Level
Understand the SB process and how it can be applied and tailored on a project. Specifically to identify:			
SB	01	The purpose of the SB process	2
SB	02	The objectives of the SB process	2
SB	03	The context of the SB process	2

Definitions

- **End Stage Report** – A report at the end of every interim management stage that the Project Manager provides to the Project Board, indicating the performance during the past stage and the project status at the moment.
- **Stage Plan** – A detailed plan used as the basis for the project management control throughout the stage.
- **Exception Plan** – A plan that is produced as a result of a threat to the agreed tolerance levels and which normally follows an Exception Report.

The objectives of the SB process (SB02)

The objectives of the SB process are:
- Assuring the Project Board that all products in the past stage have been delivered according to agreement;
- Preparing the Stage Plan for the next stage, including the agreed tolerances and the required people and resources;
- Updating the Project Initiation Documentation (and particularly the project approach), the Project Plan, the Business Case, the Strategies and the project management team with the role descriptions concerned;
- Delivering the information to the Project Board to enable the members to review the advisability, viability and feasibility of the project, including the most important risks and the

aggregated risk level;
- Recording the lessons of the past stage for the continuation of the project and/or for other projects;
- Requesting authorization from the start of the next management stage.

The context of the SB process (SB03)

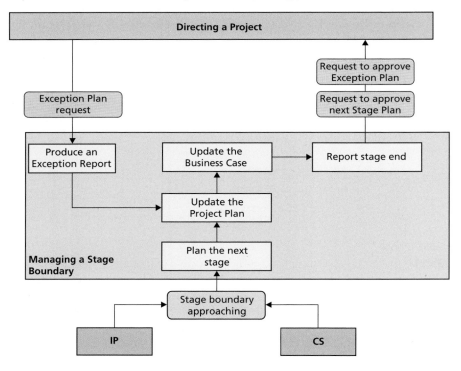

Figure 16.1 Overview of the Managing a Stage Boundary process (source: Managing Successful Projects with PRINCE2, produced by OGC)

The SB process is executed towards the end of a stage, or after reviewing an Exception Report on the basis of the direction given by the Project Board. It describes the activities undertaken by the Project Manager in preparation for a go/no go decision to be taken by the Project Board.

Normally the SB process is initiated by the Initiating a Project process in the initiation stage, or from the Controlling a Stage process for the various delivery stages. The SB process then provides the input for the end stage assessment by the Project Board in the Directing a Project process.

If the Project Board requests an Exception Plan, then the SB process is initiated from the Directing a Project process. The SB process provides the input for the assessment of the Exception Plan by the Project Board. After approval by the Project Board, the Exception Plan will replace the Project Plan or the Stage Plan, as appropriate (see figure 16.1).

How the SB process supports the PRINCE2 principles

- **Continued business justification** – The Business Case is updated to assure the continuous viability of the project.
- **Learn from experience** – Possible lessons are captured in the next Stage Plan and in Lessons Reports to the corporate or programme management, if applicable.
- **Defined roles and responsibilities** – The PMT structure and role descriptions are updated, if applicable.
- **Manage by stages** – A separate Stage Plan for the next stage is developed in conjunction with an update of the Project Plan.
- **Focus on products** – The next Stage Plan and the updated Project Plan are product based.
- **Manage by exception** – Provides a decision point for the Project Board on whether to continue or not with the project.
- **Tailor to suit the project environment** – The PID and, in particular, the project approach, the PMT and the role descriptions, are updated and the next Stage Plan and Project Plan are tailored to suit the project environment.

The activities within the SB process

The Managing a Stage Boundary process consists of the following activities:

Plan the next stage
The Stage Plan for the next stage must be sufficiently detailed to serve as the basis for the daily management of the stage by the Project Manager. The Stage Plan should contain all of the specialist and management products to be delivered in the following stage. In addition, it should contain the controls, such as the format, and the method and frequency of the Checkpoint Reports and Highlight Reports. Finally, the Stage Plan must also contain all tests and other quality activities for the stage, including the effort of people and resources required.

For products to be delivered in the next stage, the Project Manager should work with Project Assurance to establish who needs to be involved in the associated quality control activities in order to achieve acceptance of the products. The PID is updated to include any changes in areas such as quality expectations and acceptance criteria, the project approach, the strategies and controls, and in the PMT structure and role descriptions. Changes in the staffing of the project management team are ideally made during a stage boundary.

The Stage Plan for the next stage is developed, incorporating the relevant lessons from the current stage. The Configuration Item Records for the new products are created and the records for the existing products are updated as appropriate. The Quality Register is updated with the planned quality activities for the next stage. The Issue and Risk Registers are updated with any issues and risks that (may) affect the Stage Plan for the next stage.

Produce an Exception Plan (if applicable)
As soon as one or more tolerances of the stage and/or project are at risk, the project is not viable any more. In these circumstances, the Project Board can ask the Project Manager, in response

to the Exception Report received, to produce an Exception Plan based on the selected option to proceed.

The Exception Plan replaces the Stage Plan for the remaining part of the current stage. The remaining activities of the Managing a Stage Boundary process remain the same. The Exception Plan is equal to the original plan that it replaces in terms of set-up and detail. The outstanding activities of the current stage should be covered in the Exception Plan.

Update the Project Plan
The Project Board uses the Project Plan during the entire project to review the progress of the project. It is, therefore, important that the Project Plan is kept up-to-date with the actuals from the current Stage Plan, together with the forecast duration and cost from the next Stage or Exception Plan. With an updated Project Plan, the members of the Project Board are able to determine what has been achieved so far and what has still to be realized. The updated Project Plan also acts as a basis for the updating of the Business Case. An explanation of the possible changes to the Project Plan is included in the End Stage Report. The Issue and Risk Registers are updated to reflect the new issues and risks identified.

Update the Business Case
At each management stage boundary, the Business Case and the Benefits Review Plan have to be updated. With the update of the Business Case, consideration must be given to any known risks and issues, and the Risk and Issue Registers need to be reviewed accordingly. With the update of the Benefits Review Plan, the results of benefits reviews undertaken in the current stage have to be compared with the expected results.

As part of the update the Business Case activity, a risk analysis should be performed and the Risk Management Strategy should be reviewed to ensure that the project remains within the agreed risk tolerances. With the preparation of the go/no go decision at the management stage boundary, it is important that the overall aggregated risk exposure is understood as well as an appreciation of individual risks.

The Project Manager coordinates the changes in the Business Case with the Executive. The Project Manager can be assisted by Project Assurance responsible for business assurance on behalf of the Executive. If the Business Case becomes weak, the Project Board has to discuss this with the corporate or programme management.

Report stage end
In the End Stage Report, the actual results of the current stage in terms of time, costs and delivered products are reviewed in relation to the original Stage Plan and the agreed tolerances. Furthermore, the End Stage Report contains an update of the Business Case and a forecast of the project and next stage performances. In addition, a review of the team performances and the products delivered are included together with, if applicable, a Lessons Report incorporating recommendations to the corporate or programme management.

For the review of the product performance, the Project Manager may use a Product Status Account, provided by the Project Support. For reporting the stage end, the Project Manager can be assisted by Project Assurance.

If a phased handing over is scheduled, the subsequent activities of the Closing a Project process have to be carried out simultaneously. The associated follow-on action recommendations can be included in the End Stage Report.

After completion of the End Stage Report, the Project Manager requests the Board to approve the next Stage Plan/Exception Plan and to grant him/her discharge from the current stage based on the End Stage Report. The Project Manager informs the other stakeholders in accordance with the Communication Management Strategy.

The responsibilities within the activities of the SB process

For an overview of the roles and responsibilities for the SB process, see table 16.1.

Table 16.1 Roles and responsibilities for the Managing a Stage Boundary process

Corporate / programme management	Project Manager (PM)
• Confirm updated PID • Confirm updated Business Case • Confirm updated Benefits Review Plan **Project Assurance** • Review Next Stage Plan and Product Descriptions • Review and update Configuration Item Records • Review and update Quality Register • Review and update Issue and Risk Registers • Review Project Plan • Review and update Project Initation Documentation • Review and update Business Case • Review and update Risk Management Strategy • Review and update Benefits Review Plan • Review End Stage Report • Review Lessons Report and follow-on action recommendations (if required) • Review Exception Plan (if applicable)	• Create Next Stage Plan and Product Descriptions • Approve Configuration Item Records • Approve Quality Register • Update Issue and Risk Registers • Update Project Plan • Update Project Initiation Documentation • Update Business Case • Update Risk Management Strategy • Update Benefits Review Plan • Review Product Status Accounts • Produce End Stage Report • Produce Lessons Report and follow-on action recommendations (if required) • Produce Exception Plan (if applicable) **Project Support** • Produce Product Status Accounts • Create new / update existing Configuration Item Records • Update Quality Register **Team Manager (as part of MP process)** • Review and update Quality Register

Multiple choice - Managing a Stage Boundary process

SB01. The purpose of the Managing a Stage Boundary process is best described by?
a. To provide the Project Board with the correct information in order to take the decision to proceed
b. To provide a clear end to the stage and to see where we are
c. To make a fresh start by assessing the current Stage and planning the next Stage
d. To make it possible for the Project Board to prematurely close the project

SB02. Which of the following is NOT an objective of the Managing a Stage Boundary process?
a. Updating the Project Initiation Documentation
b. Recording the lessons of the past stage
c. Assuring the Project Board that all products in the past stage have been delivered according to agreement
d. Handing over the stage products to the corporate or programme management

SB03. When is the Managing a Stage Boundary process executed?
a. At a point where it is anticipated that tolerances may be exceeded
b. When the Controlling a Stage process has been completed
c. At the beginning of a new stage
d. After reviewing an Exception Report on the basis of the direction given by the Project Board

SB04. What principle is supported in the Managing a Stage Boundary process by the End Stage Report?
a. Management by exception
b. Continued business justification
c. Management by stages
d. A clear start and end

SB05. Which of the following documents is NOT an output of Managing a Stage Boundary?
a. Updated Project Initiation Documentation
b. Benefits review
c. Product Status Account
d. Updated Configuration Item Records

SB06. Fill the blank in the following sentence with the correct product.
The [?] is produced by Project Support and reviewed by the Project Manager.
a. End Stage Report
b. Risk Register
c. Product Status Account
d. Exception Plan

17 Closing a Project (CP)

Purpose (CP01)

The purpose of the Closing a Project (CP) process is to create an unambiguous moment when the acceptance of the end result is confirmed and it is established that the objectives according to the original Project Initiation Documentation and the approved changes have been realized, or the project cannot contribute anymore.

Learning outcomes

Syllabus area	Topic	Topic description	Level
Understand the CP process and how it can be applied and tailored on a project. Specifically to identify:			
CP	01	The purpose of the CP process	2
CP	02	The objectives of the CP process	2
CP	03	The context of the CP process	2

Definitions

- **User acceptance** – A formal confirmation by those who will use the project product, once it is handed over, that the project product complies with the acceptance criteria.
- **Operational and maintenance acceptance** – A formal confirmation by those who will be responsible for the operation and maintenance of the project products that the project products comply with the specifications.
- **Closure recommendation** – A recommendation to the Project Board, prepared by the Project Manager, that the project can be closed, serving as project closure notification if the Project Board agrees with this.
- **Post-project benefits review** – A review held after project closure to determine if the expected benefits have been realized.

The objectives of the CP process (CP02)

The objectives of the CP process are to:
- Verify the user acceptance of the products to be handed over;
- Ensure the operation and maintenance is in place before the project ends;
- Review the project performance against its baseline;
- Assess any benefits that are already realized and update and plan the benefits not yet realized;
- Ensure all open issues and risks are captured within the follow-on action recommendations;

• Ensure that lessons learned are forwarded to corporate or programme management by the Lessons Reports.

The context of the CP process (CP03)

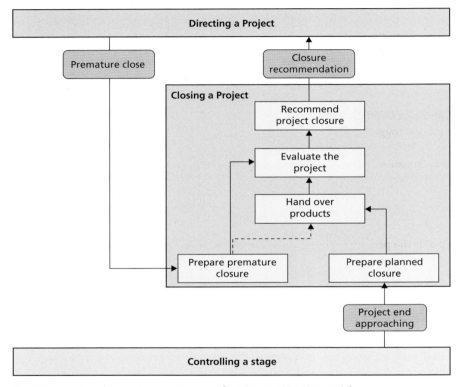

Figure 17.1 Overview of the Closing a Project process (based on OGC PRINCE2 material)

The CP process is generally initiated by the Project Manager from the Controlling a Stage process. The CP process can also be initiated by the Project Board from the Directing a Project process in a situation where there is no longer a viable Business Case and the project has to be prematurely closed (see figure 17.1).

The different activities of the CP process can be executed in parallel to each other. The activities of the CP process must be planned separately in the Stage Plan of the final delivery stage. The CP process provides the input for the assessment of the project by the Project Board in the activity authorize project closure.

A project requires a clear start and end point. Without a definite project closure point a large part of the commitment created through the formal acceptance of the results of the project can be lost. The CP process describes the activities that must be executed by the Project Manager so that the Project Board can approve the closure of the project. The progress of the project is evaluated against the baseline, ensuring that the project deliverables can be taken into use. Recommendations for follow-on actions are prepared and, in case of a phased hand-over, a check is made on the extent to which benefits have already been realized.

How the CP process supports the PRINCE2 principles

The CP process supports all seven PRINCE2 principles:
- **Continued business justification** – The Business Case is updated to form the basis for the benefits realization after completion of the project.
- **Learn from experience** – Lessons Reports are created to forward to corporate or programme management.
- **Defined roles and responsibilities** – The responsibilities for delivering the project are ended and the process triggers the responsibilities for the operation and maintenance of the project products.
- **Manage by stages** – Supports the closure and discharge of the final delivery stage.
- **Focus on products** –The focus is on handing over products according to specified quality criteria.
- **Manage by exception** – Provides a decision point for handing over products and the closing of the project.
- **Tailor to suit the project environment** – Identifies the parties concerned to be informed to suit the project environment, based on the Communication Management Strategy.

The activities within the CP process

The Closing a Project process consists of the following activities:

Prepare planned closure
Before closing the project the Project Manager has to make sure that all project products have been completed to the agreed standards. This involves the following: request a Product Status Account to verify if all project products have been approved and meet the quality criteria defined; update the Project Plan with the actuals to date; confirm the completion of the project and seek approval to notify the corporate or programme management that resources can be released.

Prepare premature closure
In some cases a premature closure is ordered. In that case the Project Manager should not just simply abandon the work, but should conserve what is valuable and arrange for this to be handed over to the corporate or programme management. The Project Manager has to record the premature closure decision as an issue in the Issue Register.

In such a situation the Project Plan also needs to be updated on the basis of a Product Status Account, and approval must be sought to notify the corporate or programme management that resources can be released. However in this case a more accurate account has to be put together about the status of the products, such as: what is not yet started, what is under construction and what has already been completed. Further, it has to be determined which products must still be secured or completed within the project or by the corporate or programme management and which products must be transferred to other projects. Finally, estimates must be prepared for the remainder of the activities. An Exception Plan must be prepared if necessary.

Hand over products

The Project Manager ensures that operation and maintenance is in place before the project is closed. The Benefits Review Plan is updated to include all post-project benefits reviews planned after completion of the project. Recommendations for follow-on actions are prepared for all activities not yet executed and for any outstanding issues and risks. The Configuration Management Strategy is examined to check how the project products should be handed over.

The Project Manager ensures that the acceptance of the project products is confirmed by the end users as well as those who will become responsible for the operation and maintenance of the products. Acceptance records must be obtained, especially when the project products have been produced by external parties. The responsibilities for the products are transferred from the project to operation and maintenance. The Configuration Item Records are updated and handed over.

Evaluate the Project

In the End Project Report the ways in which the project performed against its planned targets, tolerances and approved changes are reviewed. In addition, the End Project Report contains a review of the team performances as well as a review of the products delivered, including confirmation of the handing over of the project products and the acceptance records together with a summary of the follow-on action recommendations.

The End Project Report also contains an update of the Business Case: which benefits are already achieved, what are the benefits still to be expected and what is the forecasted deviation from the approved Business Case?

Finally the Lessons Learned Report is prepared. This focuses upon what went well and what can or must be better, and includes any recommendations for corporate or programme management. Lessons recorded in the Lessons Log are used for compiling the report. The Project Manager should seek the reflections of the individual members of the project team. The Lessons Learned Report is, by default, part of the End Project Report, but can also be a separate report.

Recommend project closure

After all preparatory, handover and evaluation activities have been undertaken, the Project Manager can close all logs and registers and can secure and archive all project documentation in accordance with the Configuration Management Strategy.

Finally the Project Manager can prepare and send a draft project closure notification to the Project Board. The Communication Management Strategy is used to identify all stakeholders who should be informed by the Project Board about the final closure of the project.

The responsibilities within the activities of the CP process

For an overview of the roles and responsibilities for the CP process, see table 17.1.

Table 17.1 Roles and responsibilities for the Closing a Project process

Project Assurance	Project Manager (PM)
• Review Product Status Accounts	• Review Product Status Accounts
• Review updated Project Plan	• Update Project Plan with actuals
• Review additional work estimates	• Produce additional work estimates
• Review Business Case	• Update Issue Register
• Review acceptance records	• Update Business Case
• Review updated Configuration Item Records	• Obtain acceptance records
• Review follow-on action recommendations	• Approve updated Configuration Item Records
• Review updated Benefits Review Plan	• Produce End Project Report and Lessons Report
• Review End Project Report and Lessons Report	• Update Benefits Review Plan
• Review draft Project Closure Notification	• Produce End Project Report and Lessons Report
	• Close Issue, Risk and Quality Registers
Project Support	• Close Daily and Lessons Logs
• Produce Product Status Accounts	• Produce draft Project Closure Notification
• Create / update Configuration Item Records	

Multiple choice - Closing a Project process

CP01. What is a purpose of the Closing a Project process?
a. Ensure that the project has nothing more to contribute
b. Ensure that the post-project benefits reviews will be carried out
c. Ensure that the project closure notification will be issued
d. Ensure that the Lessons Report will be distributed

CP02. How is the Closing a Project process best described?
a. Prepare closure, hand over and evaluate
b. Close logs and registers, hand over and review benefits
c. Notify Project Board, hand over and discharge the project team
d. Implementation, acceptance and after-care

CP03. Which of the following is NOT an objective of the Closing a Project process?
a. Verify the user acceptance of the products to be handed over
b. Ensure the operation and maintenance is in place before the project ends
c. Update the Risk and Issue Registers for handing over to the operation and maintenance
d. Assess any benefits that are already realized and plan the benefits not yet realized

CP04. When is the Closing a Project process activated?
1. When the Project Manager concludes that the final products are ready for delivery
2. When premature closure is ordered by the Project Board
3. When the project end is approaching
4. When the Project Manager concludes that the project doesn't support the Business Case anymore.
   a. 1, 2, 3
   b. 2, 3, 4
   c. 1, 3, 4
   d. All

CP05. How does the Closing a Project process support the learn from experience principle?
a. It updates the Lessons Log with the lessons learned during the final stage
b. It updates the Business Case and Benefits Review Plan for future benefits reviews
c. It creates follow on recommendations for lessons learned for the operation and maintenance period
d. Lessons Reports are created in order to forward to corporate or programme management

CP06. What is the Project Manager responsible for within the Closing a Project process?
a. Review draft Project Closure Notification
b. Obtain acceptance records
c. Produce Product Status Accounts
d. Create/update Configuration Item Records

Appendices

A.1 Glossary

Term	Description
A	
accept (risk response):	A deliberate decision not to implement any risk responses to a threat on the assumption that taking action will not be effective until the threat actually occurs.
acceptance:	The formal confirmation that the project product complies with the acceptance criteria and meets the requirements of the stakeholders.
acceptance criteria:	A list of measurable criteria which the project product must comply with before the stakeholders will accept it.
approval:	Formal confirmation that a project product is complete and complies with the criteria specified in the Product Description.
assumption:	A statement that is taken as true. Plans are based on this. This is necessary when the specific data is not available at that moment
assurance:	Systematic actions necessary to give confidence that requirements will be met and the aims realized.
authority:	The right to allocate resources and to take decisions (at project, stage as well as team levels).
authorization:	Formal confirmation that an authority is granted.
avoid (risk response):	A risk response resulting in the fact that a threat cannot occur or will have no longer an impact.
B	
baseline:	Recorded or approved status of a product or item, that, once it occurs, is subject to change control.
baseline management product:	A management product that defines aspects of the project that, once approved, are subject to change control.
benefit:	The measurable change that is indicated positively by one or several stakeholders.
Benefits Review Plan:	A plan that indicates how, when and by whom the benefits to be realized are measured.
Business Case:	The information that reflects the justification for the setting up and execution of a project.
C	
Change Authority:	The person or group to whom the Project Board has delegated the responsibility to assess, authorize and deal with change requests and off-specifications.
change budget:	The budget that is assigned to the Change Authority, intended for approved requests for change.
change control:	The procedure that ensures that all changes that can affect the objectives of the project are identified and assessed, and are approved, rejected or continued.
checkpoint:	An assessment of the progress of a project at team level, at predetermined points in time.
Checkpoint Report:	A report on the progress of a Work Package that the Team Manager provides to the Project Manager at predetermined times.

Term	Description
closure notification:	Advice from the Project Board to all stakeholders that the project is being closed and that the team members and supporting facilities are no longer required from a specific date.
closure recommendation:	A recommendation to the Project Board, prepared by the Project Manager, that the project can be closed, serving as project closure notification if the Project Board agrees with this.
Communication Management Strategy:	A description of the means and frequency of all internal and external communication from and to the stakeholders.
concession:	An exception to specification that is accepted by the Project Board without any corrective actions.
configuration item (CI):	A product, component of a product, or set of part products of which the realization and/or control must be controlled.
Configuration Item Record:	A record in which all relevant information of a configuration item is described, including the relationship that configuration item has with other configuration items.
configuration management:	The management of the configuration items (CIs), comprising planning, identification, control, status justification and verification of the CIs.
Configuration Management Strategy:	A description of how and by whom the products in a project are controlled and protected.
configuration management system:	A combination of processes and supporting software that is used to control the Configuration Item Records.
constraint:	A boundary or limit with which the project must comply.
contingency:	A budget post for activities that could not reasonably have been foreseen, but which fall within the scope of the project.
controls:	Management products or procedures to monitor progress against the allowed tolerances and to report the progress to the next management levels for information and decision-making.
corporate or programme standard:	An over-arching standard from the corporate or programme organization to which the project strategies and controls must comply.
corrective action:	An action to resolve a threat to a plan's tolerance or an off-specification to a product.
customer:	the person or group who commissioned the work and will benefit from the end results.
customer quality expectations:	A statement by the customer about the quality to be expected from the project product.
D	
Daily Log:	The (Project) Manager's diary that is used to record problems/concerns which can be handled by the (Project) Manager informally.
deliverable:	see output.
dependencies:	The relationship between products and/or activities.
dis-benefit:	The measurable change which is deemed negative by one or more stakeholders.
E	

Term	Description
End Project Report:	A report provided by the Project Manager to the Project Board at the closure of the project that confirms the handing over of the project products, the realized performance and the updated Business Case.
end result:	The entirety of the products delivered, or a synonym for 'project product'.
end stage assessment:	A review by the Project Board to authorize the next Stage Plan.
End Stage Report:	A report at the end of every interim management stage that the Project Manager provides to the Project Board indicating the performance during the past stage and the project status at the moment.
enhance (risk response):	The risk response to increase the probability and/or the impact of an opportunity.
event-driven control:	A control that is triggered by an event, for example a stage boundary, or an event within the organization, such as a year closing.
exception:	A situation in which it can be expected that the agreed tolerance levels of a plan will be exceeded.
exception assessment:	A review by the Project Board to authorize the Exception Plan.
Exception Plan:	A plan that is produced as a result of a threat to the agreed tolerance levels and which normally follows an Exception Report.
Exception Report:	A report in which an exception is described, including the (impact of the) recommendation.
Executive:	The single individual with overall responsibility for ensuring a project meets its objectives and delivers the projected benefits.
exploit (risk response):	A risk measure ensuring that an opportunity is seized and that the impact will be realized
F	
fallback (risk response):	A risk response to reduce the impact of the risk, that will not be deployed until the risk actually occurs or (as the case may be) threatens to occur.
follow-on action recommendations:	A report of recommended actions in respect of incomplete activities, outstanding issues and risks and other actions that are needed to take the product into the next stage of its product lifecycle.
G	
governance:	The duties (with the accompanying tasks, responsibilities and authorities), processes and procedures that define how an organization is set up and managed.
H	
handover:	The transfer of the ownership of the deliverable products to the user(s).
Highlight Report:	An outline report on the progress of a stage that the Project Manager provides to the Project Board and other stakeholders at predetermined times.
I, J, K	
impact (of risks):	The result of a threat or opportunity if this occurs.
inherent risk:	The size of a risk before any responses are taken.

Term	Description
initiation stage:	The first stage of a project after the approval of the Project Brief in which the Project Plan is specified and the management infrastructure of the project is designed.
issue:	Relevant unplanned event that has occurred and requires attention to resolve or conclude.
Issue Register:	A register for recording all issues that are being formally managed.
Issue Report:	A report containing the description, impact and the decisions regarding issues such as requests for change or problems that are being formally handled.
L	
Lessons Log:	An informal log in which the lessons are recorded for the current and future projects.
Lessons Report:	A report that documents any lessons that can be useful for other projects.
logs:	Informal recordings of data, managed by the Project Manager, that do not need any approval from superior management as regards lay-out and presentation.
M, N	
management product:	A product that will be required as part of managing the project, and establishing and maintaining quality.
management stage:	A division of the project in time, with previously defined activities and deliverables, that is managed by the Project Manager under the authority of the Project Board.
milestone:	A significant event in a plan's schedule (for example the delivery of specific Work Packages, or the end of a technical or management stage).
O	
off-specification:	A project product that (as expected) does not comply with the specifications or has not been/is not being delivered.
operational and maintenance acceptance:	A formal confirmation by those who will be responsible for the operation and maintenance of the project products, that the project products comply with the specifications.
opportunity:	An uncertain event that could have a positive impact on objectives.
outcome:	The result of change, normally described in terms of the way in which it affects real-world behavior and/circumstances.
output:	A specialist product that is delivered to the user(s). It can be a product as well as a service.
P	
performance target:	A specific target of a plan in respect of time, cost, quality, scope, benefits and risks.
plan:	A detailed proposal for achieving a result or an aim which specifies who undertakes what, where, when and in what way.
planning horizon:	The time period for which an accurate and reliable plan can be produced.
post-project benefits review:	A review held after project closure to determine if the expected benefits have been realized.

Term	Description
premature closure:	The closure of a project sooner than planned when all the products to be delivered have not yet been achieved.
prerequisite (plan):	A fundamental aspect that must be in place before a plan can be taken into operation.
PRINCE2:	A method that supports some selected aspects of project management. The acronym stands for PRojects IN a Controlled Environment.
probability:	The likelihood of a risk occurring.
problem/concern:	Issue that is not a request for change or an exception to the specification and that the Project Manager needs to resolve or escalate.
procedure:	A series of actions that must be executed in sequence for a specific aspect of project management.
process:	A structured set of activities that are designed to accomplish a specific objective.
producer:	The person responsible for the realization of a product.
product:	An input or output of a process or project, whether tangible or intangible, that can be described in advance, created and tested.
product-based planning:	A technique that leads to a comprehensive plan based on the creation and delivery of required outputs.
product breakdown structure:	A hierarchical summary of all requirements and products to be produced during a plan.
product checklist:	A list with the most important products of a plan, plus key dates in their delivery.
Product Description:	A description of a product, comprising among other things the aim, the composition, the origin and the quality requirements of a product.
product flow diagram:	A diagram with the production sequence and the time sequence dependence of the products which are listed in a product breakdown structure.
product lifecycle:	The total time spans of a product from the original idea, via creation, use and, ultimately, replacement or dissolution of the product.
Product Status Account:	A report of the status of products.
programme:	A temporary flexible organization structure, created to coordinate, direct and monitor a set of related projects and activities in order to deliver outcomes and benefits that contribute to the organization's strategic objectives.
progress:	The measure of the achievement of the objectives of a plan.
project:	A temporary organization that is created for the purpose of delivering one or more business products according to an agreed Business Case.
project approach:	A description of the manner in which a project result will be approached.
Project Assurance:	The responsibilities of the individual members of the Project Board to ensure that the project is executed in the correct way.
project authorization notification:	A notice from the Project Board to all stakeholders and to the site where the project activities will be undertaken, that the project is about to start, requesting all required services to be made available during the project.

Term	Description
Project Brief:	A statement that describes the purpose, performance requirements and constraints of a project, to obtain authorization from the Project Board to start the initiation of the project.
Project Initiation Documentation (PID):	The collection of documents that contains the key information needed to start the project on a sound basis and that conveys the information to all concerned with the project.
project initiation notification:	A notice from the Project Board to all stakeholders and to the site where the project is to be undertaken that project initiation is to start, requesting all required support services to be made available during the initiation.
project lifecycle:	The total time span of a project from the start up to the acceptance of the project product.
project management:	The planning, delegating, monitoring and control of all aspects of the project, and the motivation of those involved, to achieve the project objectives within the expected performance targets for time, cost, quality, scope, benefits and risks.
project management team:	The total of all persons who fill the management roles in a project.
project management team structure:	An organization chart showing the people assigned to the project management team roles to be used, and their delegation and reporting relationships.
Project Manager:	The person given the authority and responsibility to manage the project on a day-to-day basis to deliver the required products within the constraints agreed with the Project Board.
project mandate:	An external product generated by an authority to commission a project, which triggers the starting up a project process.
project office:	A temporary office set up to support the delivery of a specific project.
Project Plan:	A high level plan that shows the management stages and the most important products of the project, when it will be delivered and at what cost.
project product:	What the project must deliver to be accepted.
Project Product Description:	A special type of Product Description about the project product, that defines what the project must deliver in order to gain acceptance
Project Support:	An administrative role in the project management team.
proximity (of risk):	The time period in which risks can occur.
Q	
quality:	The totality of features and inherent or assigned characteristics of a product, person, process, service and/or system that impacts on its ability to show that it meets expectations or satisfies stated needs, requirements or specifications.
quality assurance:	An independent check that products comply with requirements and are 'fit for purpose'.
quality control:	The process of monitoring specific project results so that they comply with the relevant standards, and of establishing ways to eliminate causes of non-compliance and unsatisfactory performance.
quality criteria:	A description of the quality specifications with which a product must comply, including the quality measurements that will be applied by those inspecting the finished product.

Term	Description
Quality Management Strategy:	A strategy defining the quality techniques and standards to be applied, including the different responsibilities for achieving the required quality levels during a project.
quality management system (QMS):	The complete set of quality standards processes, procedures and responsibilities for a site or organization.
quality records:	Evidence kept to indicate that the required quality assurance and quality control activities have been undertaken.
Quality Register:	A summary of all the planned and completed quality activities. The Quality Register is used by the Project Manager and Project Assurance as part of reviewing progress.
quality review/ inspection:	A systematic and structured assessment of a product that is carried out by two or more selected people in a planned, documented and organized fashion.
R	
record:	Dynamic management product that maintains information regarding a project's progress.
reduce (risk response):	A proactive risk response to reduce the probability and/ or the impact of a threat.
request for change:	Request to change the baseline of a product, process or condition.
register:	Formal repository of data managed by the Project Manager that require agreement by the Project Board on their format, composition and use.
reject (risk response):	A deliberate decision not to implement any responses to an opportunity on the assumption that taking action will not be effective until the opportunity actually occurs.
release:	The specific set of products in a handover. See also 'handover'.
report:	Management products with which the status of certain aspects of the project are recorded.
request for change:	A request to change the baseline of a product, process or condition. It is a type of issue.
residual risk:	The risk remaining after a risk response has been applied.
responsible authority:	The person or identity who is authorized to initiate the project and to commit funds.
reviewer:	An independent person or independent group that assesses products on the basis of the criteria specified in the Product Description.
risk:	An uncertain event or set of events that, if it arises, has consequences for the achievement of objectives.
risk actionee:	A nominated owner of an action to address a risk.
risk appetite:	The attitude of an organization towards the taking of risks.
risk assessment:	The appraisal of the possible likelihood and impact of the individual risks and of the aggregated risk.
risk estimation:	The estimation of the probability and impact of an individual risk.
risk evaluation:	The assessment of the net impact of the threats and opportunities on an activity when aggregated together.
Risk Management Strategy:	A description of the goals as well as the procedures and techniques of applying risk management and the reporting requirements.

Term	Description
risk owner:	A named person who is responsible for the management, monitoring and control of a particular risk assigned to them.
risk profile:	A description of the types of risks which an organization faces and its exposure to those risks.
Risk Register:	A register of the identified risks, including the corresponding status and history.
risk response category:	A subgroup of risk responses.
role description:	A description of the tasks, authorities and responsibilities for a specific role.
S	
scope:	The sum total of the deliverable products and the extent of their requirements for a plan.
Senior Supplier:	The Project Board role that provides knowledge and experience of the main disciplines involved in the production of the project's specialist products.
Senior User:	The Project Board role for ensuring that user needs are specified correctly and that the solution meets those needs.
share (risk response):	An agreement between two parties to share the positive as well as the negative impacts of risks (a threat or an opportunity) by means of a pain/gain formula.
specialist product:	A product whose development is the subject of the plan.
Stage Plan:	A detailed plan used as the basis for project management control throughout the stage.
stakeholder:	Any person, group or organization that can affect, be affected by, or perceive itself to be affected by, an initiative (project, programme, activity or risk).
start-up:	The pre-project activities of the Executive and Project Manager to prepare the outline Business Case, the Project Brief and the Initiation Stage Plan.
strategy:	An approach or line to take in order to achieve long-term goals.
supplier:	The person or group(s) responsible for the supply of the project's specialist products.
T	
tailoring:	The appropriate use of PRINCE2 on any given project, ensuring that there is the correct amount of planning, control, governance and use of the processes and themes.
Team Manager:	The person responsible for the production of the specialist products allocated by the Project Manager, according to the agreed Work Package, to an appropriate quality, timescale and at a cost acceptable to the Project Board.
Team Plan:	An optional level of plan for the delivery of a Work Package.
technical stage:	A method of grouping work together by the set of techniques used, or the products created.
theme:	An aspect of project management that must be applied mandatorily and continuously, and that requires specific treatment for the PRINCE2 processes to be effective.
threat:	An uncertain event that could have a negative impact on objectives.
time-driven control:	A management control that is triggered by a moment in time.
tolerance:	The permissible deviation above and below a plan's target.

Term	Description
transfer (risk response):	The transfer of the negative (financial) impact of a risk to a third party.
trigger:	An event or decision that initiates a PRINCE2 process.
U	
user:	The person or group(s) who will use one or more of the project's specialist products.
user acceptance:	A formal confirmation by those who will use the project product once handed over, that the project product complies with the acceptance criteria.
V	
variant:	A configuration which slightly differs from the original.
version:	A specific baseline of a product. Versions commonly use naming conventions that enable the sequence or date of the baseline to be identified.
W, X, Y, Z	
Work Package:	A (set of information relevant for a) subset of the works to create one or more products.

A.2 Foundation examination candidate guidance

This format explains the format of the question papers and the types of questions asked.

Every candidate receives:
1. Question Booklet, on which the multiple choice questions are provided.
2. The Answer Sheet, on which your answers must be given.

Style of questions

There are four different test styles used within the paper.

1. Standard	2. Negative	3. Missing Word	4. List
Which response type is recommended for opportunities and threats? a) Reject b) Share c) Avoid d) Reduce	If the Project Board does **NOT** provide a decision, to whom should the Project Manager defer? a) Executive b) Change Authority c) Project Support d) Project Assurance	Identify the missing words in the following sentence. The Quality theme provides procedures that ensure that the [?] created meet the needs of the project. a) plans b) products c) Project Board d) controls	When checking the status of a Work Package, what does the Project Manager look at? 1. Checkpoint Reports 2. Mandate 3. Quality Register 4. Team Plans a) 1, 2, 4 b) 2, 3, 4 c) 1, 2, 3 d) 1 ,3 ,4

In the Foundation paper five negative, five missing word and five list questions will be used. All other questions will be standard style questions.

Use of the answer sheet

There will only ever be one answer to each question. If more than one answer is given in the answer sheet the response line will be void and will attract no marks. Marks are not subtracted for incorrect answers.

The Answer Booklet will be read electronically and the results generated by computer. It is therefore essential that candidates follow the instructions given and mark their answers accordingly.

If candidates wish to write their answers on the question booklet first, they must be aware of the additional time needed to complete the answer sheet. Only answers submitted on the answer sheet will contribute to the result.

The candidate has to answer the questions by filling in the 'oval' that relate to their chosen response. The oval must be filled in IN PENCIL, NOT PEN. If a pen is used, the answers will not be marked.

The only acceptable ways to complete the answer sheets are (see figure G1):
• Completely filling in the oval
or
• Drawing a line through the centre of the oval.

Figure G.1 Acceptable ways to complete the answer sheet

Any other method, including ticks or crosses, is **not** acceptable and may not be marked. If a candidate wishes to change their answer during the exam, the incorrect answer should be erased completely and the correct answer indicated. The question will score zero if more than one answer is given.

All 75 questions should be attempted.

A.3 Multiple choice answer key

Answer Key		Answer Key		Answer Key		Answer Key		Answer Key		Answer Key	
Q.	Ans.	Q.	An	Q.	Ans.	Q.	Ans.	Q.	Ans.	Q.	Ans.
OV01	A	QU01	A	RK07	B	PG07	C	IP05	A	SB05	B
OV02	D	QU02	C	RK08	D	PG08	B	IP06	B	SB06	C
OV03	A	QU03	B	RK09	B	PG09	C	IP07	B	CP01	A
OV04	B	QU04	D	RK10	C	PG10	A	IP08	D	CP02	A
OV05	C	QU05	C	RK11	C	PG11	B	CS01	D	CP03	C
OV06	D	QU06	B	RK12	B	SU01	A	CS02	B	CP04	A
OV07	D	QU07	A	CH01	A	SU02	B	CS03	C	CP05	D
BC01	C	QU08	B	CH02	D	SU03	C	CS04	D	Cpo6	B
BC02	A	QU09	A	CH03	A	SU04	B	CS05	A		
BC03	A	PL01	A	CH04	B	SU05	C	CS06	C		
BC04	D	PL02	B	CH05	A	SU06	A	CS07	C		
BC05	A	PL03	C	CH06	D	SU07	D	CS08	D		
BC06	A	PL04	A	CH07	B	DP01	B	CS09	A		
OR01	D	PL05	D	CH08	C	DP02	D	MP01	A		
OR02	D	PL06	A	CH09	C	DP03	C	MP02	C		
OR03	C	PL07	A	CH10	C	DP04	A	MP03	D		
OR04	B	PL08	B	PG01	A	DP05	C	MP04	A		
OR05	B	RK01	A	PG02	C	DP06	C	MP05	B		
OR06	C	RK02	A	PG03	D	DP07	A	MP06	C		
OR07	A	RK03	C	PG04	D	IP01	A	SB01	A		
OR08	B	RK04	C	PG04	D	IP02	C	SB02	D		
OR09	C	RK05	B	PG05	B	IP03	C	SB03	D		
OR10	D	RK06	C	PG06	B	IP04	B	SB04	B		

A.4 Organizations

APMG International Offices
APMG-UK – www.apmgroup.co.uk
APMG-Benelux – www.apmg-benelux.com
APMG-China – www.apmg-china.com
APMG-Deutschland – www.apmg-deutschland.com
APMG-Scandinavia – www.apmg-scandinavia.com
APMG-US - www.apmg-us.com
APMG-Australasia – www.apmg-australasia.com

Best Practice User Group UK – www.usergroup.org.uk
PRINCE User Group Netherlands - www.pugnl.nl
PRINCE User Group Germany - www.prince2-deutschland.de
Other project management organizations
IPMA – www.ipma.ch
APM – www.apm.org.uk
PMI – www.pmi.org

A.5 References

Managing Successful Projects with PRINCE2™, 2009 Edition
This English manual contains the official description of the PRINCE2 method of managing projects:
Author: Office of Government Commerce
Publisher: The Stationery Office
ISBN: 9780113310593

Managing a Successful Project Using PRINCE2™, Syllabus 2011
APMG, 2010

PRINCE2™ Foundation Exam Candidate Guidance V1.2

Projectmanagement op basis van PRINCE2® Editie 2009
Bert Hedeman, Hans Fredriksz, Gabor Vis van Heemst, 2009, Van Haren Publishing, Zaltbommel, The Netherlands, ISBN 978-90-8753-495-0

PRINCE2® 2009 Edition, A Pocket Guide
Bert Hedeman, Ron Seegers, 2009, Van Haren Publishing, Zaltbommel, The Netherlands, ISBN 978-90-8753-544-5

A.6 About the authors

Bert Hedeman is a senior project and programme manager, who worked abroad for many years. Bert is an accredited PRINCE2, MSP, P3O and MoP trainer and co-author of the books 'Project Management based on PRINCE2™ Edition 2009', 'Programmamanagement op basis van MSP, Editie 2007' and 'Projectmanagement op basis van NCB versie 3'.

Steffi Triest's current occupation is Management Director at Semcon Project Management GmbH. She has got 20 years experience in adult education in the IT-industry and has been working in the field of Project Management for many years in different roles and countries. Steffi is an accredited PRINCE2 trainer, certified as a PMP®, founder and current president of PMI Berlin/Brandenburg Chapter. She has been the Chair of Translation Verification Project for the German Version of PMBOK® Guide 3rd and 4th edition. She is Co-Author of the book "Das PMP-Examen – zur gezielten Prüfungsvorbereitung" and publishes articles regarding Project Management on a regular basis.

Gabor Vis van Heemst is director of intrprimus project en programme management. Intrprimus is a home for experienced project and programme managers who are specialized in 'making change work' for our clients. Gabor is helping organizations to professionalize their business and increasing the added value of changes. He is a experienced manager, consultant and trainer with a passion for aligning the goals of people with the goals of the organization and using this to drive them forward. His dream in every assignment is to make the wanted change visible and tangible for all stakeholders. He makes projects fun again!

Index